BEST OF THE BEST

Lead Boldly, Scale Rapidly, Create Your Legacy.

IVY SLATER

#1 International Best Selling Author

BEST OF THE BEST:
Lead Boldly, Scale Rapidly, Create Your Legacy

Copyright © 2025 by Ivy Slater

RHG Media Production
21519 Knoll Way, Castro Valley, CA 94546.

Paperback ISBN: 979-8-218-62898-7

Visit us on line at www.YourPurposeDrivenPractice.com

Published in the United States of America.

WHAT PEOPLE ARE SAYING

"You won't want to put this down once you start."
—**Frank Rekes** – Partner & Financial Planner

"It is a powerhouse guide for leaders eager to elevate their businesses and lives. Her emphasis on visionary leadership, confidence-building, and strategic financial planning resonates long after you've turned the last page."
—**Frank King** – The Mental Health Comedian

"Best of the Best is a must read as it captures the essence of Ivy's wisdom and practical strategies that will profoundly impact how you lead. Highly recommended for anyone seeking to grow both personally and professionally."
—**Kelly Rittenberry Culhane** – Managing Partner & Chief Growth Officer, CM Law

"By reading Best of the Best, I promise you will learn to build a business that fulfills your hopes and dreams."
—**Leslee Cohen** – Founder All Rise Legal Counsel

"Ivy Slater's new book, "Best of the Best" is worth its weight in gold, heck platinum!!!!!

From the first few pages until the last, get ready for a treat. Success is for those willing to do the work and play at a higher level while also building a life of their dreams."
—**Precious L. Williams** –CEO, The Perfect Pitch Group

Table of Contents

HOW – AND WHY – TO USE THIS BOOK

When I sit down with a new client, I ask them this question: *What is your vision for your personal life in the next 5-10 years?*

After we explore the answers together, this is my next question: **How can your business complement this vision?**

Then we do the numbers.

In all my years running my businesses and helping other leaders run theirs, I have found that if you build the business without aligning it with what brings joy and meaning to your life, you will end up spending all your time and energy ON the business. And you will struggle to stuff your life in and around the nooks and crannies that are left.

Both your business and your life will suffer.

I am here to say that you can have BOTH!

Imagine designing your business on your own terms so that your life flourishes from your business and vice versa – while you **grow and scale your company to legacy levels.** This is what it looks like to be "the best of the best" professionally and personally. And this book gives you a roadmap to get there.

My approach is comprehensive and multi-pronged, using the best of leadership soft skills and hard skills:

- Reinforce the business fundamentals that too often are swept under the rug as the everyday push takes over and settling on the status quo feels easier.
- Do the inner work to become the best version of yourself as a Visionary Leader, influencer, professional brand, deal closer and rainmaker. Move from the idea space to the action space – do the numbers, assess, analyze, adjust, and ACT.

Within these pages you'll find:

- Concepts explained and illustrated with the valuable advice of experts
- "Ivy's Office Hours" that puts the concepts to work in real time with my clients
- "Visionary Action Steps" to use in practice and make some meaningful, measurable shifts in the way you do business – right away
- Worksheets at the end of each chapter to embed what you've learned and share with your leadership/exec teams

These are the kinds of business- and lifestyle-building gems that I talk about with my client CEOs and execs all day every day – sensible, often simple steps to take that so many people aren't aware of, forget, or avoid because they are so steeped in the demands of their everyday business that they don't stop to look up at what's possible.

The bottom line: You build a great business to live a great life. Who you are as a person with meaning and vision in your life and what your company can become are part of the same equation. *100%.*

So, here is your chance to step off the hamster wheel, direct your attention to YOURself and what YOU want in your business and in your life, and allow me to guide you through.

It will be my honor and privilege. Let's go!

***

On a bright, crystal-clear morning in autumn my husband Michael offered to drive me to work on his way to his office in Brooklyn. He dropped me off near Timothy's Coffee Shop a few blocks away from my office.

I got my regular nonfat latte and took my familiar morning walk through Times Square to my office. As a matter of habit, I glanced up at the iconic giant billboard screen at 1560 Broadway, expecting to see the "The Today Show" broadcast like I always did.

Instead, I saw an image that soon the whole world would not forget: A plane crashed straight into the World Trade Center sending dark, billowing smoke and fire out into the sky.

My knees buckled and I sank down to the curb on Seventh Avenue, still clutching my coffee. In that moment, everything stopped as people saw that image – impossibly, you could hear a pin drop in the middle of Times Square. As the incredible image I'd just witnessed registered, my brain began to be bombarded by a million thoughts ....

Where is my husband? Are my children okay? How do I get to them? Where are my people right now and how are they doing? I need to reach out to my staff ... my business partner ... my mom who was probably at my office right now ... clients who might be on their way or, worse still, could be inside that tower building at this very moment ....

... How do I keep everyone safe?

Anything that had to do with work, money or deals disappeared – it was all about loved ones and my people. Nothing else mattered. It was time to take action to make sure they were safe and supported.

I looked up, and there was Michael. He had also seen what happened and had circled back with the car to find me.

Step #1: Get to our home. We ran to the car and pulled out into slow-to-dead-stop traffic, people in the streets either running in panic or wandering in a state of collective shock, first responders screaming past in their emergency vehicles. We inched forward toward our apartment which was barely a mile away – so close, yet so far.

My husband and I are business leaders. We were used to making decisions on behalf of others who depend on us. So, we jumped into decision-making mode. First I made calls to the school to make sure our two young children were safe and plans were in place for them to return home once all the parents had been notified. Then I called my people while Michael did the same for his.

At home now, with one landline and spotty cell service (because the mono-poles had been located on top of the Twin Towers), I finally reached my partner at the office, and we agreed that the group would walk uptown through Central Park to my apartment where we would gather and support our clients, vendors and each other. To my relief, my mother, Rita, was among them so she would be safe (she was our part-time bookkeeper).

Michael put an announcement on our answering machine for anyone who might call: *This is Ivy and Michael, if you need a place to come, you know our address. Our doors are open.* That might sound crazy in today's world but we felt the desire to support those who might need help.

Our children were safely home now, and we realized we'd better get food, as who knew how many people would be with us, how many stores would stay open, and – the most fearful thought – what else might happen to endanger our city that would have us hunkering down in the days ahead?

I took our first-grade son to the pizza place around the corner. The street was eerily empty because apparently public traffic had been diverted to one of the main streets in order to allow full access to the emergency vehicles going downtown toward the Towers. As we walked amid the steady stream of sirens blaring, I held my son's hand tightly, his eyes opened wide as saucers.

What a stark contrast to those screeching sirens when we entered the pizza place. There was a long line, and it was quiet and somber. We all waited silently, together in the line.

A woman walked in to take her place behind us. She was covered from head to toe in ash. People began to turn to her and in almost one single gentle voice say, *Are you okay? Where are you coming from? What do you need?* She said quietly and wearily, "I was downtown and I'm trying to walk home to the Bronx because all the subways are shut down." Streets were closed. New York City was locked down. She had been walking for hours – the World Trade Center was 13 miles from her home.

Of course, everyone escorted her to the front of the line. She only wanted water, but people said, *Give her food, I'll pay for her, I'll pay for it*. Everyone wanted to pick up the bill. The guys behind the counter calmed us down and said, "Thank you, everybody, there is no charge for her. Nobody needs to pay. We'll take care of her." With a lot of well wishes exchanged, we got our pizza and left for home.

***

Being smack in the middle of the World Trade Center attack brought into stark focus some lessons that have stuck with me through the years, into my work today as an executive business coach and consultant with Slater Success.

Here are three of them which you will see threaded throughout *The Best of the Best*, because they are fundamental to a leader's success in their business as well as personal life.

1. Your company is only as good as your people – and they're everything.

One of my clearest memories of that time, and one I'm very proud of, is how our company came together as a team with the clear, common purpose of service to our clients and community and to each other. My team and I worked tirelessly and selflessly that afternoon and in the weeks to come, as an entire city and country joined to move through the trauma and start the wheels of work rolling again.

Making fast decisions – ready or not – defined this momentous day. And these decisions came down to what was most important in our lives: Human connection is so much more valuable than how much money is in the bank account.

Taking care of people and being of service to others is what keeps business alive – and what makes a business thrive financially.

Any plan I make with my clients today is with the human connection element in mind, and we know that it's an integral part of the success they achieve. I've witnessed again and again how product, marketing, finance, tech, and operations alone do not make a company profitable.

It's the people who make success happen! People are the lifeblood of any business, and the best of the best will pay attention to this precious asset!

2. Do the numbers, make the best decisions you can make at the moment, and move on.

Ever since I was a teenager, my parents taught me: Know your numbers, do the numbers, find the value in your company, and never shortchange yourself. My father was CEO of a successful company. My mother started her own interior design business when I was in elementary school and later in life went on to be a business manager of a film editing company.

On that fateful September day, I was CEO of Slater Graphics. I knew our numbers, I'd orchestrated a merger that gave us five years of next-level growth, we had added the latest printing industry technology, and I had a team I trusted completely.

I felt confident that I had a handle on my business. We were solid and able to withstand just about any challenge. I can't stress enough how reassuring it was to know these things during one of the most devastating events that could happen in one's life.

Were we perfect? No. Did I make misjudgments? Definitely. All I could ask of myself as a leader was to do my due diligence, make the best choices with the best information I had at the time, and then move on without regrets.

When we make decisions, particularly at business inflection points, we rarely have all the answers. What we want to ensure are the fundamentals of our business model and structure, controlling what we can count on and having a plan for what we can't.

3. Meet the world as it is – and create your future in it.

No matter how much we plan, schedule and envision, life happens and the world changes. You'll read stories in this book about leaders who have adapted to unexpected circumstances (like a global pandemic), who have made courageous changes in their careers to create a new future, or have challenged the status quo with a new way of doing business – and won.

We hope to have control over those changes, but it's not always so. It's the challenging times that test our mettle – and often even greater opportunities are waiting on the other side if we're able to grab them.

My father, Irving Slater, and I had been working side by side in the printing industry for almost ten years before I started my own company. Life was great in New York City – my family and I lived in a terrific apartment in the heart of Manhattan, going to shows, dining out, travelling often. By all of society's standards, I was successful. I had it all, right?

Then, one Spring day I lost my father. He collapsed on a Saturday and passed the next day.

In typical Ivy style, I jumped into "crisis can-do" mode, making arrangements for my company to open as usual on Monday without a hitch, then the logistical arrangements for my father's funeral. I stubbornly shunned help and dug in my heels to do it all myself.

I took exactly one week off and then got right back into caring for my husband, children, my now-widowed mother, and a seven-figure business.

During the next several months I never gave myself the space to grieve. I just rallied on, continuing to take care of my family and to build the business, gain new corporate clients, make capital improvements, and seal new deals.

The first anniversary of my father's death also happened to be the eve of my 45th birthday. I was in the middle of taking care of some last-minute details for my birthday party when, without warning, I simply imploded!

I cried and cried like there was no tomorrow. And it continued for days into weeks on end.

Anytime, anyplace, the tears might start to flow – *except in front of my family, employees or clients*. I was strong enough to do what was needed, then fell apart later.

Of course, I didn't see it at the time, but now I know I had been trying to hold everyone and everything together like Atlas' bent body shouldering planet Earth. What a burden I had taken on! In the midst of my responsibilities to everyone else, I had forgotten myself.

I was an emotionally out-of-control mess – still running my business and maintaining my composure when I needed to, but how long would that last? Every day was a challenge and a burden.

At the same time, thoughts and questions began to swirl through my head. Eventually I started paying attention to them – or, more accurately, I couldn't escape them:

> *Was I going to die a printer (it wasn't my dream)?*
>
> *What else could I do (with my current skill set)?*
>
> *What is my legacy (beyond wife and mother)?*
>
> *Twenty years in this business and I'm running out of steam (again, not my dream).*

> *There HAS to be something more for me (my work is not bringing me joy).*

The protective shell I had constructed for myself after my father died was beginning to crack. I had BIG ideas. I yearned to do something meaningful and helpful to others. I wanted to do business from a place of joy and purpose.

Seventeen years ago, when I joined Slater Graphics (then Slater Lithography), I saw the world in front of me and the future I wanted for myself, so I grabbed the opportunity that would take me forward. I've never regretted that choice.

Yet now I realized that I loved the relationships I had built through Slater Graphics, but I didn't love the industry itself. The skill set I excelled at and loved most was communicating with people, encouraging them, inspiring them, coaching and cheerleading them on to help them get things done and meet their goals.

Over the years people had often sought my counsel on their business, to help them think through major decisions or how to navigate a growth transition. One colleague suggested to me, "You're going to become a coach – you're already doing it! You helped me see the vision and potential of my business. Suggested some shifts and opportunities that were effective when implemented. And today I offer a range of options to work with clients and am making much more money!"

The shell cracked open a little more. I began to see more clearly the world I was in – an experienced business owner, middle-aged with children soon to leave the nest, and consumed with the urge to do something I would love that was also lucrative. In that moment, I accepted that THIS was the person I am now, and began to open my eyes to the opportunities before me in this "new" world I wanted to create.

So, as scary as it was, I changed my career at the age of 45. I left a great-paying CEO position with two children to support in college and a Manhattan lifestyle I enjoyed – to enter a new, then relatively unknown field. I became certified as a business coach and founded Slater Success in 2008.

Today I am running a business that supports my financial goals, my lifestyle, and my personal legacy vision – and has set me on a journey of exploring the best of the best in Visionary Leadership.

I see in my work how easy it can be to limit our perspectives on what our life looks like and the opportunities before us. We can get stuck in ONE way of approaching our careers, business strategies and life itself.

From the unexpected situations I've faced and the adaptations I've made over these years, my can-do attitude and, yes, my stubbornness when it comes to striving for the best, I have the ability to walk my clients through *the process of seeing WHO they are, WHERE they are, WHAT they want to create for their business and themselves, and HOW to see opportunities they may never have imagined. And get them implemented.*

This is what I want for you to gain from *Best of the Best: Lead Boldly, Scale Rapidly, Create Your Legacy.*

And to love every minute of the journey!

CHAPTER ONE

UNLEASH YOUR INNER VISIONARY

"You have to have a vision so big that you're willing to walk through a wall for it."

—**Joe Curcillo,** Strategic Advisor with
Generalist's Advantage Strategies LTD[1]

Business leaders all have the ability to be visionaries. So, what distinguishes the best of the best – the Whitney Wolfe Herds, Warren Buffetts, Walt Disneys, Oprah Winfreys, Jeff Bezos, Cynthia Marshalls, Bill Gates – from the "average" leader?

They can see the future and make it happen.

Visionary Leaders are typically defined as people who have a clear picture of what they want in the future, and inspire others to join them in making that vision a reality. Yet, I see very smart and capable *business leaders who haven't yet stepped into BOTH the ability to see their big-picture vision AND use the practical skills to implement that vision for their business.*

The place to start? Uncovering your own Inner Visionary.

If you can't see where you are going with clarity, passion, and alignment with your desires, then how can you expect to succeed in making the plan, maintaining the momentum, and inspiring others to join you?

How your Inner Visionary leads you to guaranteed growth:

- ***Charges up your personal power*** which drives everything you do to lead the way to achieve your vision. "Personal power" is not the position you hold; it's an attitude of confidence, strength, and self-mastery.
- ***Sets you apart from the others*** because you are tapping into and leveraging *your unique* combination of imagination, wisdom, and creativity – you make things happen like nobody else does. Your vision-forward thinking breaks free from "how we've always done it" and your vision is so clear that you don't worry about what others think.
- ***Electrifies your relationships*** because you become that person people are drawn to – a person who shows up confident, trustworthy and likable; knows their values and priorities; shows strength and clarity in their decision-making. People want to hitch their wagon to your star.

Clearing the way to uncover your Inner Visionary

What could be stopping you from unleashing your own visionary power, uniqueness, and magnetism? What stops most leaders is this: **They get caught up in the day-to-day running of their business.**

The daily preoccupations and worries cause stress, which blocks their ability to lift their head above the fray to see the big picture they're working so hard to achieve. They are keeping busy being busy – *but they're not being productive and definitely not growing.* And if the stress and worry continue, productivity continues to suffer which brings the company farther than ever from achieving their goals.

You can see the vicious cycle. Why does this happen, even to our most capable leaders? For most of us it's more comfortable and safer to keep our head down – because the alternative is looking ahead to the unknown. *Very uncomfortable.*

The Future's Unknown.
Take The Leap Anyway.

Imagine this: You're on a huge roller coaster that's housed inside an even huger building. All the lights are out so you see *nothing but pure blackness.* You're sitting in the narrow car and it starts inching up and up and up. You don't know how far it's going to go up, or when it's going to hit the top and the start racing downward. Scary, right?

Businesses are like roller coasters, rising and falling, ebbing and flowing. That's the nature of growth. Uncertainties are inevitable. Nothing's guaranteed.

People who fear the unknown cannot picture a vision for themselves and their business. They resist change, stay in the weeds, and their business (and lives) stagnate.

Your Inner Visionary requires you to be ready to face the unknown even if you're feeling uncomfortable in the dark. You face whatever comes and make the best decision you can make at the time. At times you might just feel like you're on a free-falling roller coaster.

Yet you see what's possible, and you don't shy away from the decisions you need to make to push through the unknown and onto that exhilarating ride.

Now, I'm not recommending the "jump off a cliff and build your parachute on the way down" way of running your business! **The Inner Visionary + Implementation = Success.** 100%. I'll talk more about achieving your goals through data, numbers, strategies and measurable results in these next chapters.

Let's start with your Inner Visionary game …

SPOT THE HORIZON BEYOND THE EVERYDAY GRIND.

As the leader's thoughts get consumed by those everyday concerns and activities, they lose sight of their end goals – often including their very quality of life ... until circumstances stop them in their tracks and force them to "look up."

I know many business owners who keep pushing through until they literally crash and burn – as you know from my story, I was one of those people.

The experience woke me up, I saw the lesson in my burnout, and made a commitment to change things for myself. I had my vision in my sights, and made decisions (some risky, some scary) to move toward that vision, all bringing me to the thriving business I have and love today!

My vision keeps my focus on the horizon so I don't fall back into getting buried again in the everyday tasks and narrow outlook.

The first step is to clear the way for your Inner Visionary to emerge. This is a matter of looking beyond your current thinking to really view the horizon and see the possibilities ahead. Only then can you articulate a vision powerful enough to lead your business to become the best of the best.

Visionary Action Step #1:
Take the leap and visualize your future.

All of your business decisions become a matter of choice, not force.

Schedule some dedicated time to get off the roller coaster, step back, and take an honest look at your relationship with the future:

1. ***Look at your everyday grind in a different light.*** Ask yourself these vital questions. Get honest yet compassionate with yourself as you answer:

- *What am I sacrificing by holding onto my current way of handling everyday concerns and activities?*
- *Have I lost sight of my bigger-picture goals/vision in my "busyness"?*
- *Am I stalling our business growth by avoiding big decisions that have to be made for our future direction? If so, what are those decisions?*
- *Could I be keeping busy just to avoid future risk? If so, what am I afraid of?*

2. **Expand your thinking about your situation** as you answer these questions, and begin to look for creative possibilities and solutions. You may want to work on this with a trusted advisor or even your exec team to flesh out some new perspectives.

3. **Consider one thing – right now – that you could do differently** to free yourself up to be less "busy" and more "productive" to move forward. List three realistic options, and choose one to start working on today!

HOW TO BE THE TORTOISE *AND* THE HARE.

There's one type of client I call a "slow mover." They run their business, steady and focused on the fundamentals like payroll, rent, etc. Fine! Yet they are slow to realize that change is needed for their business to grow – or even to survive. When I introduce some changes that could move them forward, the response is: *We're not ready yet.* They tell me my ideas are good, and they'll address them "soon."

Because the slow mover procrastinates or avoids taking action, the business often gets forced into making a quick decision that ends up riskier, costlier and more anxiety-producing than if they'd made a timely decision.

Ivy's Office Hours: Founding partner Benjamin came to me with concerns about hiring for his IT services firm. Business was building fast and he could see they needed more people. He was getting pushback from some of his partners wanting to put off taking any action. (Guess what they said? You got it: *We're not ready yet.*)

When we started working together, the business was in crisis mode, unprepared for an emergency that threw everyone off while the deadlines kept piling on.

In our coaching call, I explained the "slow mover" concept, ending with: *Ben, it sounds like you have some good ideas here, and a good sense of what your company needs to do in this emergency situation. What do you think is holding your partners back?*

Ben: *I'd been thinking it was that typical "'tech startup founder" mentality, but our business is ten years old now and we should be past that. Now I understand what's probably behind the pushback is that at least a couple of the guys could easily be described as the "'low mover" type.*

Actually, I'm so relieved because I've been worried that they'll never get past that startup mentality. You're helping me see that a solution might be possible!

Me: *What slow movers often need is a powerful way to be convinced about the decision you're suggesting. These people need some strong data to make the case for a decision they can wrap their heads around. One thing I believe is this: The numbers don't lie!*

Ben and I worked together on the numbers to support the net value of outsourcing the hires, as well as some growth scenarios to help feed their Inner Visionary. We then framed the conversation with the partners.

They came onboard and within a few months the necessary positions had been filled – without wasting any more of their time, money or angst. Ben reported back that things not only were going a lot more smoothly; the partners had begun conversations on investing in the firm's growth.

Does this mean that it's better to be a quick decision maker? No, not always. I also see clients who rush into decisions for various reasons that are not good for the business.

Do you recall Aesop's fable about the race between a tortoise and a hare? As the story goes, the fast hare gets so far ahead of the tortoise that he decides to take a nap. The tortoise, slow and steady, finally passes the hare (who's still fast asleep), and the tortoise wins the race.

My moral to the story? Be both! Strike a balance between the slow, steady tortoise and the fast ready-for-action hare.

Clearing the way for your Inner Visionary to emerge means you become discerning and informed about the decisions in front of you – through a steady, future-thinking foundational process. Then you take action when the time is right and without hesitation or procrastination. A balanced approach wins the race!

Visionary Action Step #2:
Think like the Visionary Leader who
will make the future happen.

When your future begins to take shape more clearly, your mind opens up to the opportunities and possibilities in front of you that will create that future. You might realize at this point that things have to change – probably starting with yourself as a leader.

Who do you have to become to create this amazing future you are envisioning?

> *"The biggest thing you can learn is to go from DO-er to LEAD-er. This means empowering your team so your time is freed up to pay attention to the future."*
> —**Kevin Wolf,**[2] *CFO at American Financial Exchange*

1. ***Open up your mind to the reality of change***, so you can dissolve the fears or anxiety you might have around it. Accept the truth that there's

a risk to decision-making – as well as the risk of inaction. No decision is still a decision! Your goal is to make good decisions from a place of control, whether you tend to identify with the tortoise or the hare.

2. ***Answer these questions:***

- *What's my current risk tolerance level and what might I want to change about that?*
- *Am I making decisions from a place of control, strength and clarity? Or are any emotions getting in the way?*
- *How am I making, or not making, decisions that are aligned with my business goals and vision?*

3. ***Choose a decision you have to make***; practice inviting both the hare and the tortoise to the table. Study the options, do a risk-benefit analysis, take your best, clearest look at the situation. If you find yourself getting stuck here, don't be afraid to ask for support – from your team, outside experts, and others you trust. Then ... decide and move on.

What it takes to unleash your Inner Visionary

Here are four game-changing steps to unleash your Inner Visionary which I've used to grow my own businesses as well as take my clients to multimillion-dollar success.

STEP #1:
UNLEASH YOUR ATTACHMENT TO THE WAY IT'S ALWAYS BEEN.

Run your business from where you are going, not where you are. This is a mindset that will take you out of stagnation in a hurry. It will accelerate your plans to achieve your success goals and reach your vision.

If something's not working, it's because you need to change how it's done – or stop doing it. It's that simple: Address what's not working now and don't wait 'til "someday."

This takes thinking a different way to get a better result, one that's aligned with your business goals and vision.

Visionary Action Step #3:
Think forward with fresh eyes about what your
business could look like in the long-term.

Think unconventionally, poking holes in the way things have been done before. Allow your Inner Visionary to open your eyes to new ideas and possibilities. Look at:

- What's working well now
- What's not working well now
- Where the gap is between where you are now and where you want to be
- What adjustments you can make to reach your vision of the future

My colleague, Dr. Willie Jolley, was a popular and award-winning jazz vocalist in the 1980s. "I was flying high," he says, "billing the number one spot in a jazz club ... nice home, sports car, all of it."

When an unexpected circumstance upended his career, Willie was forced to re-imagine his life and current way of doing things.

What did he do? He took time to explore and uncover his Inner Visionary. As a result, Willie risked everything to become a motivational speaker, founded Willie Jolley Worldwide, earned his doctorate, and today is a global thought leader, Hall of Fame speaker, popular radio and television personality, and author of several international bestselling books, including his best-known, *It Only Takes a Minute To Change Your Life*.[3] He says, "What I'm most proud of as a leader is making the decisions to not let anybody else determine my destiny."

STEP # 2:
UNLEASH YOUR FUTURE VISION –
AND CREATE *THAT.*

You know the expression "go big or go home?" Visionary Leaders don't have tunnel vision; they open their minds, see possibility, and play BIG.

When I start with a new client, I interview them about their business. AND I ask them about their age, their kids, lifestyle, interests and the legacy they want to leave. I help them picture their life years from now and how their organization is going to fulfill that life. Then we start building their success from this information.

Even though I'm a numbers person all the way, the Visionary Leader's success goes way beyond the numbers to become the best of the best. **My vision is to help my clients prepare NOW their life NOW for the joys of the future, in their personal as well as professional life.** We work together to do the numbers and business strategies to make that happen.

The Visionary Leader wants it all, financial success, meaningful impact and influence, and a fulfilling life and lifestyle!

The way to see your vision clearly is to begin to ask yourself: *How do I see myself in three, five, or ten years?* To help answer, think about:

- Amount of years you see yourself working full-time
- Where and how often you want to travel
- How large a company you want to build
- The foundation you want to create for global change
- What you want to leave to your kids or community

Let your imagination take you to those places. ***Everything is creatable.***

**Visionary Action Step #4:
Get very, very specific about your goals.**

Goals are an integral part of the vision you create. You know this, and you also know how often we create goals and don't meet them. As a Visionary Leader who wants a different outcome, try this:

- Think of your vision and what goals or outcomes you would need to complete so you could realize that vision. Focus on three to five goals, and get into the details.
- If you want to make money, decide on the number. Write it down. Decide the time frame – how many dollars in how many months or years? Write it down. If your vision is a home (or running a business from home), what does it look like? Where is it? How many rooms? Get that down in writing.

When you set down your goals in writing, they become more impactful because they are embedded in your brain.

- Once you have a set of goals that you're happy with, make them your "law" – that's what I call them. ***I write my goals into law***, so they are unbreakable. That's how important they are to my vision and success.

STEP #3:
UNLEASH YOUR X FACTOR. YOU HAVE ONE. USE IT. FLAUNT IT.

You have at least one noteworthy special talent or quality that is the reason why people choose to work and be with you instead of anyone else. When you put these qualities together, you have the *X Factor*, that unique and indescribable thing that makes you stand out. Name it charisma, magnetism, or force of nature – whatever it's called, ***it's your own personal type of mastery. Your particular brand of personal power.***

"Sometimes being a little bit country and a little bit rock and roll gives you a different way of looking at things that gets the problem and sees the solution."
—**Mary Ann Pierce,** *Founder and CEO of MAP Digital*[4]

We talked earlier about the combination of imagination, wisdom, and creativity that's uniquely yours. These are the qualities you'll leverage to create and execute your vision. Then you take your X Factor and connect it to the vision you're going to create. Everything you do will have your one-of-a-kind stamp on it, your personal brand. The sky's the limit on what you can create!

I recently updated my X Factor, with friend and business consultant Sarah Victory,[5] who noted something about me that I had downplayed for decades. I live in Manhattan, the heart of NY. I love this city and everything it offers culturally – dance performances, theater, amazing assortment of top-notch restaurants and night spots to choose from, the architecture, the museums. I love to experience what is, for me, the best of the best! It's such a natural thing to me that I never noticed it's part of what makes me unique.

As I've embraced my X Factor I'm more fully comfortable with whom I am in my business connections and my team. Not only does it feel really great, I also see how people respond to me more clearly, and how we find common ground immediately as I share things I'm passionate about and that are important to me. It's magic – and has brought me new, fantastic clients!

Visionary Action Step #5:
Unleashing your X Factor requires curiosity and exploration into who you are and what you are passionate about.

Diving deep like this may take a bit of bravery and self-compassion. I know you're up to the task. Your first assignment is to complete the "25 SPECIAL

QUALITIES" worksheet you'll find at the end of this chapter. Open up and have fun!

STEP #4:
UNLEASH YOUR "HUMAN" SIDE.

Vulnerability wins. Show your human side (and, by the way, the X Factor will undoubtedly appear). Showing who you truly are doesn't take away your competency as a professional or leader – it actually can enhance it.

1. ***Showing your human side makes you relatable, trustworthy, and likable*** – the keys to building and sustaining lucrative connections that will grow your business.

Bottom line: People do business with people, not companies. If they are going to be vulnerable enough to devote their precious dollars, time, business brand, and future success to someone, they sure want to know they can trust them and relate to them.

So, no matter what service you provide or industry you are in, you want to open yourself up to being known by others – and that takes vulnerability.

1. ***Show your human side to your company and teams.*** If you want your people to support your vision and goals along the way, be vulnerable (without giving over your leadership power or authority). How does it work? In simple, thoughtful ways, such as:

   - When you need to take time off for family or other personal things, let your team know about it openly and *without apology* (I know many leaders for whom this is very difficult).
   - In turn, show up in full support of your team's time and life outside the office. Let a team member take a flex day – you'll know they need it because you've gotten to know them, and you sincerely want their needs to be met. They will return their appreciation with more engagement and motivation.
   - Take 100% responsibility for your decisions and your mistakes. Masking your mistakes actually shows your weakness rather than

your strength. Your team will notice you're doing it – trust me, they know ....

Visionary Action Step #6:
Change your take on "mistakes."

We have been programmed all our lives to see mistakes as failures, and to see vulnerability as a weakness. Reframing your take on mistakes is a powerful exercise. When I changed my definition of mistakes it changed everything about my success.

Try this on: *Mistakes are just something to add to my learning curve.* Shift the word "mistake" to the term "learning curve" whenever the word comes up, or choose an alternate term that works for you.

- Now practice that concept, starting with small wins. Faced with a "mistake," don't judge but look at the lesson in it. What can you take from it to make a change for the better? Where does this move you forward on your learning curve to become the best of the best?
- Then move on – this is key. No regrets.
- Get open and vulnerable and teach your people what you've learned. Then everybody has more information and it's a win for all.
- Next, work on supporting your people and teams on their learning curve. Help them see the lesson and let them figure out new solutions. And watch the results happen!

Unleashing your Inner Visionary: TAKEAWAYS

Leveraging your Inner Visionary is the key to Visionary Leadership.

- You have a clear picture of what you want in the future, and inspire others to join you.
- Your personal power charges you up and drives everything you do.
- You are tapping into your unique combination of imagination, wisdom and creativity to make things happen that nobody else does.

Your Inner Visionary comes through when you clear out old ways of thinking.

- The future is unknown; don't avoid it. Face – and create – your future with the support of your strong vision.
- Take yourself out of the everyday minutiae to look beyond your current thinking.
- Shift bad decision-making habits to a balanced approach. Make all of your decisions a matter of choice, not force.

Unleash and leverage your Inner Visionary to become an exceptional Visionary Leader.

- Run your business from where you are going, not where you are.
- See your future vision with fresh eyes, and create THAT. Everything is creatable.
- Tap into that unique and indescribable thing that makes you stand out – your X Factor.
- Vulnerability wins. Show your human side, and support others in showing theirs.

25 SPECIAL QUALITIES + TALENTS WORKSHEET

INSTRUCTIONS: Write down 25 special qualities and talents you possess – yes, 25. It will make you dig down to come up with that many, and you may find yourself going far beyond that number. If so, go for it!

If you get stuck, look at your client testimonials to see what they say about you – they know best! Write down the words and phrases they're using. Step into these qualities. Practice "flaunting" your X Factor. Watch the positive responses.

1. _____

2. _____

3. _____

4. _____

5. _____

6. _____

7. _____

8. _____

9. _____

10. _____

11. _____

12. _____

13. _____

14. _____

15. _____

16. _____

17. _____

18. _____

19. _____

20. _____

21. _____

22. _____

23. _____

24. _____

25. _____

CHAPTER TWO

THE POWER OF PURE PROFIT

*"Financial knowledge is power. Be empowered
and find the advice you deserve."*

—**Stacy Francis,** CEO of Francis Financial
and Founder of Savvy Ladies

A s a Visionary Leader, you seek to evolve. You look to what will take your business to the next level, a new era, and the next million(s). Integral to pursuing your vision is to understand what success really means in terms of profitability.

It takes tapping into the power of pure profit!

To understand "pure profit" let's get clear on the terms *profit* and *profitability,* as they can mean different things to different people. And both give insight into different aspects of your business.

***Profit* describes your business gains** after you subtract your expenses, in absolute amounts, which show on your income statement. In your business, do you describe profit as:

- The dollar positive gain after you've subtracted expenses?
- The earnings that flow to investors?
- Whatever you have left at year-end that you can invest?

***Profitability* analyzes more than income** – the relationship between your revenue and expense to see how well you are performing financially, as well as your potential for growth. You look at different profitability ratios to see if your business is earning enough profit to sustain and grow. The common profitability measures are:

- Profit margin ratio
- Gross margin ratio
- Return on investment ratio

***Pure profit* is typically described as the "accounting" profit,** the numbers your books show plus taking into consideration the *implicit costs,* such as the transfer costs of management, depreciation, insurable risks, overhead expenditures, and similar obligations which occur but aren't usually shown as a separate expense.

The game-changer for my clients' success is that I add **one more factor into the Pure Profit Equation: *building vision and opportunity into your profitability picture.*** This is what I call the power of pure profit.

You get a *complete picture* of your business now and what it can look like in the future. You create this fuller picture and work with it on an ongoing basis throughout the year, so you know where you stand at any given moment and are prepared to meet the opportunities (and risks) when they arise.

> *"Bring in that discipline and thought process so that if there is an M&A, PE or outright acquisition opportunity, you are ready to have that conversation."*
> —**Aditya Mishra,** *General Partner of BAT VC*[6]

Does your current version of reaching your vision include:

- Basing your profitability on sales alone?
- Looking at investing in growth only as long as you have "leftover" money at the end of the year?

- Leading with managing debt as your business model rather than leading with growth?
- Postponing exciting opportunities until you "have the cash" to pay for them?
- Paying yourself last?

If any of these points are true for you, then **you're missing out on the opportunity to achieve your personal and professional vision and add millions to your company faster.**

What I'm about to share with you are methodologies, mind shifts and small but powerful tweaks in your financial strategy and financial forecasting – that the best of the best already know!

Three keys to knowing exactly where your money is going

Numbers tell a story – are you reading the book?

Bottom line: Know your numbers. I always think of my father's sage advice: "If someone asked you right now to take out a piece of paper and rough out your expenses, sales, account receivables and projections on what is in your pipeline, could you do it?"

As a leader, you must have a basic knowledge at all times of what is going on with your company from a financial standpoint. It's a proactive approach, not Monday morning quarterbacking. You cannot wait for your CFO to get back to you if a quick decision needs to be made. Always have this knowledge at your fingertips.

More leaders should trust the stories their numbers tell instead of making decisions by going with their gut, following procedures and protocols that have worked in the past or letting inertia carry them through their fiscal year!

To know your numbers means:

- You know your profits – not just your sales because your sales do not necessarily mean you're making money. This may seem obvious but I find that, particularly in professional services companies, leaders don't pay attention to this important concept.
- You know your profitability – the relationship between your current numbers and whatever profit-margin measure you've set up.
- You have your pure-profit picture in front of you.

KEY #1:
CREATE SEPARATE ACCOUNTS TO ACCOUNT FOR EVERYTHING.

When I started out as an entrepreneur back in my 20s, I divided out my accounts into commissions, savings, capital expenditure, taxes, etc. It was an intuitive move back then; I still do it today and advise my leaders to do it as well. Yes ... separate accounts (I promise it won't make your bookkeeper crazy once they see the beauty of this method!).

Everything should go through an operating account because it's logical, it's clean, and just makes sense as a way to always see how your money is working for you, or what you have to do to make it work for you.

> **Lauren, head of a 40-employee architecture firm,** hired me to help them grow their business from the plateau they were on. I worked with the leadership team on a five-year plan, and soon found they were not adequately on top of their numbers. How could they grow if they didn't know what that looks like? We began by instituting my pure-profit financial system which included creating a pure profit operating account like I've just described.

> With those numbers in front of them, they were able to understand exactly where their money was going, make adjustments to their billing, and reset quickly when things would begin to get off-track. Within two years of using my methodology, not only did they land their first seven-figure deal, they were able to pay down some debt plus devote 50% funding toward a move to bigger offices.

Visionary Action Step #1:
Set up accounts that work for YOU.

1) *Set up separate accounts that are relevant* to your particular business.

- Work with your leadership team, financial advisors, and tech people to set them up. Why? They are the experts and can help you understand how the systems can work together most effectively – no "silo thinking" here!
- Design your records to serve your current business *as well as the one you want to grow into.*

2) *Have an account for (or at least dedicated line items for) your implicit costs* I mentioned earlier. These are the kinds of expenses that often go under the radar, and silently add up to skew your bottom-line profitability. They typically show up as:

- Cost of doing business such as bank fees, subscriptions, licenses, memberships, etc.
- Little expenditures that aren't tied to client billing, or are seen as too small to capture (but they add up!).
- Non-monetary costs that sap time from yourself or your employees in ways that cost the business in missed opportunities and in actual dollars.

By accounting for your implicit costs, you'll see a longer-term picture of their effect on your bottom line. Then you can look at the activities that are actually improving your profitability and drop those that aren't – immediately.

Example: If networking is part of your business marketing strategy, have you ever kept track of the costs involved? How high are the dues? How many lunches, coffees, etc., have you paid for this year? Has it been worth it?

In the early stages of Slater Success, I felt like I was spending a lot of time and money on networking and memberships. So, I did the numbers and focused on discerning about the potential revenue I could receive from networking compared to my investment. In one instance, a $500 outlay over two years brought in a $200,000 client – good investment? I'd say yes!

3) *Plan ahead for your tax payments.* I've helped numerous clients who had not paid attention to their taxes and, year upon year, were getting caught short when the bill came due; they had to drain their savings or other accounts to pay. You cannot grow or scale (or position for sale) a company that way.

My solution: Always keep a separate fund for your taxes, and work closely with your tax accountant, bookkeeper or CFO to manage that fund so you are on top of all your tax payments.

4) *Set aside savings – yes, you can!* I advise – to the surprise of and resistance from some of my clients – that they set aside 10% of their weekly revenue into their savings account.

If you can't do 10% at first, do 5%; if you can't do it every week, try every month at first. It will make a difference, I promise you. This is where you'll find capital for projects like marketing materials, website redesign, or research for a new product opportunity. This is how Lauren built their funding for the bigger offices.

Your objectives:

- Develop saving as a habit, whatever percentage and frequency you choose.
- Stick to your commitment, whether you have a month or quarter that's flush with cash or not.
- Look at the broad picture and future growth to invest in, as the Visionary Leader that you are!

KEY #2:
YOUR FINANCIAL RECORDS TELL THE STORY OF YOUR BUSINESS – READ THEM REGULARLY.

You are my client, you are a Visionary Leader, and you want to make money. The first thing I'm going to tell you is this: ***Make it your personal commitment to look at your accounting records weekly.***

Why? Because the numbers don't lie! Your accounting records tell the story of your business health at any given moment:

Cash flow offers a bird's-eye view of income, expenses, depreciation of your net income, payroll accounts, and working capital such as receivables. Allows you to make sure you can meet all monthly obligations.

Profit and loss gives a snapshot of your company's income minus expenses during a specific period of time, like quarterly. Allows you to project earnings and see if your business-growth plan is on track.

Sales shows you when sales are up, when there's a dip, if there's a pattern to the numbers and, most importantly, what the upward trajectory looks like. Allows you to make decisions on how to grow those numbers in a sustainable way.

Price point tells you what it takes to produce and sell your product/services, factoring in overhead, implicit costs, payroll and sales tax, and other costs that will affect your bottom line over time. Allows you to ensure there's alignment between your pricing and the profitability you're projecting.

The story these numbers tell should inform every decision, large and small, that you make for your business. Period.

Once you set up your pure profit financial system – *and use it on a regular basis* – you will be able to:

- See where your money is at any given time so you can move it where it's needed most throughout the year.
- Stop the scarcity mindset of:
  - » Saving all year just to pay taxes.
  - » Never hiring because you believe you can't afford it.
  - » Stretching out your debt payments instead of chipping away steadily.
  - » **Paying yourself last because you think there's not enough money.**

- Know clearly what you need to do to keep on track with your growth game plan, whether it's to expand your sales team, shave your overhead costs, diversify your offerings, widen your client base, raise your prices, make a capital investment in growth, etc.

KEY #3:
FIND THE RIGHT ACCOUNTING AND LEGAL PROFESSIONALS – AND USE THEM.

I want it to be clear that I am not a professional financial expert. I am not a CPA, CFO, or attorney. The practices I'm describing are based on running successful businesses for over 25 years, and applying my experience and know-how to help my clients (and you) power up your sales, build your team, add millions to your company faster – in short, become the best of the best.

My companies have survived getting shut down during 9/11, Hurricane Sandy, the global pandemic, and so many other major bumps in the road.

I didn't accomplish all this alone. I counted on the expertise of my CPA, business attorneys, and CFO to help me steer my business in the right financial direction, which has helped me come out the other side of crises whole and often better than before.

Visionary Action Step #2:
Find the best of the best professional support.

You'll see in the following that I'm not just talking about the process and due diligence of effective hiring. I mean how you use your expert advisors in a proactive and strategic way as part of your growth team.

1) *Vet and select the accounting and legal professionals* (and, of course, your CFO), to make sure you can depend on them to:

- Be aligned with and supportive of your vision and business plan.

- Take an active role in reporting and translating the meaning of your numbers.
- Inform and educate you so you can confidently understand exactly where your business stands.

2) *Tap into their expertise to inform your team's decision-making.* Considering that it's the nature of legal and financial professions to be risk averse, leverage your experts' ability to take a critical look at your business plan from a financial perspective. You want to welcome "devil's advocate" input to help you and your leadership team assess all the factors before making big-ticket decisions. Better to know now than when it's too late, I always say.

Equipped with this expert and objective information, you can do the risk-benefit analysis that will set up your growth game plan for success! Now, having said this, remember ...

3) *Ultimately, YOU are the one steering the ship* – you are the Visionary Leader who sees what's ahead, welcomes new ideas and opportunities, takes risks to get where your vision leads you, and are of course accountable for the success (or failure) of your firm. You are responsible for knowing the financial numbers within your business and for directing your financial team.

Do involve your financial and legal partners: Touch base with them at least quarterly or twice a year; let them know where your business is, what you are doing, and what your vision is so they have a good basis from which to advise you.

Profit and growth:
It's the same conversation,
part of the same vision

I often come across CEOs who feel their company is growing when they're making money, and they avoid having the growth conversation when their profit is dipping in a certain month or quarter. Their thinking is, *If we're making money we're growing.* This may be true in the present moment but the year-end numbers could tell a different story.

The danger of this thinking is that leadership makes short-sighted, hit-or-miss decisions – *Let's do more of this; let's throw more money at that* – which come from overconfidence when times are flush, or from fear and panic when times are lean. In my experience, **these kinds of decisions never turn out to be good, sustainable, long-term investments in their business growth**.

Are you throwing darts at a dartboard blindfolded, or are you thinking like a visionary?

The Visionary Leader wants to KNOW! You want to know where your company is and where you're going to take it – the whole jigsaw puzzle put together, not a myopic look at all the different pieces scattered about in the box lid.

How do you think like a visionary?

Look at your particular situation (you'll have your accounting system running smoothly to give you the clear, big-picture story, right?), explore the different avenues in front of you, make case scenarios, and weigh the options. Then, **make reasonable choices by looking at the numbers, the data AND the vision.**

Many of the leaders I work with fall into one of two camps: One type wants to jump in with the vision but no data; the other keeps looking for more data until they've waited too long to take advantage of the opportunity right in front of them.

The balanced approach is the visionary way. I tell my clients, "Let's look at the vision. Let's look at your operating budget and debt. Let's look at any market research you've done, and test the market. Then make a reasoned decision."

Ivy's Office Hours: I'd been working with my client Joe to set up their numbers and Business Growth Game Plan for the upcoming year. We regularly reviewed their numbers to make sure they were on track. It's July and we're assessing the year so far.

Me: *Joe, the numbers this year have been up and down but inching steadily forward. That's great! It shows you're on the right track, and with a few tweaks you could move faster. I want to recommend this to you: I've found that you're currently pricing below marketplace levels, so I want to see you raise your prices and invest in a good marketing campaign to promote it. We know the market's there – let's meet it!*

Joe: *I don't think we have the money – our mid-year numbers are too low right now to meet our year-end goal.*

The big-picture number story had me convinced that if they followed my advice they would exceed their year-end numbers. I did my best to defend my case, but Joe wasn't having it – the data wasn't selling him. So, we tabled the idea.

Fast forward to our December financials meeting, looking at November's to-date numbers. They showed the company was positioned to exceed its goal for the year – by almost the exact amount I predicted (yes, I'd read their numbers book!).

Me: *This is great news, Joe! Any thoughts on this as you look over the year we've been planning?* (I knew he was chewing on something)

Joe (with a sheepish grin): *Well ... Ivy, I owe you an apology. I knew what you told me was a good idea, but I couldn't picture it. I see now that it was a relatively small investment that in fact we could have afforded. I wish I hadn't waited so long to act – this was a lost opportunity!*

Aha! moment – now Joe understood how the bigger picture works. We then began our profit-and-growth conversation in earnest. We created a new game plan that increased his yearly number by $750,000, and included practical medium- and long-term investments to make it happen.

The most rewarding result for me was that Joe had completely shifted his mindset about profit and growth, and his Visionary Leadership took his company to meet their higher projected numbers that next year and beyond.

Visionary Action Step #3:
Create a process for making major financial decisions.

It might look like this:

1. Tap into your Inner Visionary to invest in the future, coming from your genius zone, trust in yourself, and make sure it's a little outside your comfort zone. That's where calculated-risk decisions originate and where real growth results.

2. Meet with your leadership team with the sole agenda of the decision you want to make.

3. Outline the parameters you need to set in order to make a good decision.

4. Collect the data and do the research (always bring in the appropriate experts to help).

5. Test out two or three case scenarios.

6. Set a time limit to make the decision. Stick to it, making the most rea-soned decision possible to invest in your future needs with the info and goals you have identified.

7. Set up the strategies and actions to support that decision. Then go!

The most misunderstood factor in the Pure Profit Equation: Debt

Debt is not a sign of failure – it's an important aspect of doing business.

In my humble opinion, debt is a four-letter word that should be treated with more respect. For many companies, dealing with debt has a terrible connotation. If words have energy – and I firmly believe they do – *debt* is an energy drain that holds us back!

If you want to harness the power of pure profit, you have to change that perception. Let's look at what debt really is.

We invest in things we want to have, and we don't invest to lose money. Even if we put our vacation on a credit card to be paid off, that's acquiring debt. Sure, I would love to pay for my vacations upfront, but if I choose not to go because I don't have the cash on hand at the moment, I may miss an opportunity for a once-in-a-lifetime experience, or a good travel deal I shouldn't pass up.

And some things we invest in are immeasurable but no less valuable. Example: I know that if I take that vacation, that mental break, I will come back as a better businessperson because I'll be rested, more clear-minded, and have more creative energy to be of greater service to my business. That's a valuable ROI for myself and my company.

Expand this individual concept to the things you can do for your business that have the potential to improve it, expand it and achieve your vision for it. The concept of debt can range from:

- Going for that vacation.
- Setting up an on-site presence to service a long-term client.
- Investing in an equipment lease or capital improvement.
- Buying a new office building or plant.
- Raising capital by issuing bonds.
- Engaging an expert on succession planning.

NOTE: There are advantages to acquiring debt as well as drawbacks. The amount and type of debt that is healthy for a company to carry will vary from business to business. Always consult your tax, legal, and financial experts to investigate the pros and cons before entering into any kind of debt/loan agreement.

Visionary Action Step #4:
Do not be afraid of debt.

Being scared of debt neuters the Visionary Leader.

Taking reasonable steps to incur and manage debt means you are taking control and investing in your future growth.

> *"You can't always control the inputs.*
> *You have 100% control over your reaction to them."*
> —**Jennifer Yousem,** *Founder and CEO of I Heart EBITDA*[7]

You are making growth happen on your own terms. Another advantage I see is this: When you have control over your debt within the Pure Profit Equation, you pay off your debt more efficiently and at the same time you are still saving.

Visionary Action Step #5:
Make debt part of your pure profit picture and vision.

Your goal is not to 'tolerate' the debt factor – it's to include it as part of the full picture of your business.

1) _Include the debt factor as part of your calculus_ whenever you're having the profit and growth conversations and looking at the numbers, data and vision. The holistic decisions you make as a result will keep you in control of your growth path – with everything to look forward to and a minimum of surprises to throw you off track.

2) *For the debt you have now, use the numbers* from your different operating accounts to determine what percentage you can move into paying that debt monthly.

When your most important investments are the human ones

There's nothing that can hurt a company more than running a team who is consistently overworked and undervalued. Your people are your greatest asset and investment. Period.

When it comes to hiring and recruiting, the visionary way to go is the profit and growth conversation. However, too often the typical short-term, scarcity-driven thinking is:

> *Do I really need to hire more people?*

> *It costs me money and I don't see the money I'm making from it.*

Many people, especially in the professional services industry space, are worried about hiring. It is going to cost them money and it's tough to see the ROI. A major reason for this thinking is that they are not calculating their time – its value and its cost – into their numbers story.

> **I encouraged Elise to add a Customer Service Coordinator** to her financial advisory firm. She was concerned, telling me: "How is this going to work? That hire will have no billable value, they'll be 100% supported by our profits – where's the growth in that scenario?"

> Happily, she trusted me and hired a coordinator. Two months later, in one of our coaching calls Elise told me she hadn't realized how much responsibility she had had that was now being taken off her plate!

The partners picked up at least three hours a week to focus on business development (I had advised her to track their time so she had the numbers to measure the value of the hire). The book-keeper picked up an hour or two per week, which has allowed the leadership team more time to get a much better handle on their profit and growth numbers (which of course would help feed the next profit and growth investment decision).

Visionary Action Step #6:
Use this formula to financially assess your hiring needs.

I'm using the sample of a law firm, but the formula works for any business:

The position we're talking about is an Office Manager, and we want to assess what activities the attorneys are responsible for, how much time these activities (interruptions to their work) are taking, and what this time is costing the company.

1. How attorneys make money, whether it's a subscription or package for-mula, is on a dollars/hours basis. Plug in your number. Let's say the average is $500/hour.

2. Research shows that, on average, an employee will be interrupted some-where around five times *every hour* by having to do things that aren't directly related to their job![8] And it's not just the interruption itself, it's also the time to deal with the interruption, and then the time to get back to concentrating on the task at hand.

We tend to think of interruptions by people, coming in and out or calling, asking for something from us. Yet here is the biggest disruption of our day: the many forms of communication that constantly stream to us. From email to project apps to slack messages to social media to text messages – all of these shift our concentration and cost us more hours and money than we can imagine.

Pull your own stats by having your people do time-tracking for one or two months. Outline the specific activities they're going to track, including:

- Preparing a document for the mail
- Grappling with online meeting software
- Calls and pings back and forth with the travel agent
- Scheduling their own client appointments
- Making deposition arrangements
- After getting interrupted, getting back into the flow of the important work they've been hired to do
- Dealing with online communications throughout the day

3. The formula is simple. Let's say you're getting 3 interruptions an hour; each one is 10 minutes long. In an 8-hour day, that's 240 minutes, or 4 hours per day. Five days a week equals 20 hours.

At $500 an hour, the total cost of those interruptions equals $10,000 per attorney, per week.

Multiply that number by 48 weeks per year (accounting for holidays and vacation) and you get $480,000. For a five-person firm the dollar value of all that wasted time becomes $2.4 million!

4. Assess what this means to your company. The salary of an Office Manager who would field those interruptions is what fraction of the 2.4 million dollars?

Let's say the salary for an Office Manager is $60,000 plus benefits. The investment in this position would represent a 2% investment of that 2.4 million dollars you are currently losing to wasted time.

Other questions to consider:

- What other responsibilities could this position take on that would save you even more time and money?
- How else could you use that $2.4 million from the productivity loss? A bigger year-end bonus or raise for everyone? Expand your office space? Pay down debt?

You have just exercised the power of pure profit! By taking a piece of your business that's often overlooked, tracking and assessing it with data, and then fitting it into the holistic picture of your vision of growth, you are now in a position to make some significant and powerful forward-motion decisions.

The Power of Pure Profit: TAKEAWAYS

Tap into the power of pure profit from a holistic, visionary perspective.

- Pure profit includes four key aspects of your organization: Revenue and expense; implicit costs; profitability; and ability to build vision and opportunity.
- Know exactly where your money stands by designing the financial records that will track all the numbers you need to know to achieve your growth game plan.
- Develop a proactive relationship with your financial professionals to leverage the power of moving your money to achieve your vision.

Have the profit and growth conversation to make the highest-value, visionary decisions for your business trajectory.

- Profit and growth are both part of the same vision. Use both to make sound decisions for the present and the future.
- The balanced approach to investment is to look at the numbers, the data, AND the vision.
- Work closely with your leadership team to form informed, forward-thinking, calculated-risk based, full-picture plans for your growth.

Shift the idea that debt spells "failure" – It's part of the Pure Profit Equation.

- Embrace the mindset that debt is not a sign of failure; it's an essential aspect of doing business and growing.
- You could miss important opportunities if you wait until you have the "cash." Do the numbers, weigh the options, and make a sound decision – without delay. The ROI will come.
- Take control of managing your debt and how you pay it off. Use my accounting methodology as a big-picture tool to incur debt that's right for your company, pay it off more efficiently, AND build your savings.

Understand that your most important investments are in your people.

- Your people are your greatest asset and investment. Don't burn out your people when you are growing, or it will come back to stifle your growth.
- See how the individual puzzle pieces work together to create the whole, i.e., how a new hire can pay for itself in reducing wasted time and increasing productivity.
- Make it a regular exercise to: assess when the time is right to add to your staff (using my hiring-needs formula); look at your numbers to anticipate the growth in your business that will need more and/or different talent; and keep on top of what actions to take that will support your people to be full participants in your company's vision.

FINANCIAL DECISION MAKING WORKSHEET

INSTRUCTIONS: Use this template to make major financial decisions. Make notes on each item and check off completion.

☐ Tapping into my Inner Visionary.

Notes on what I want to invest in, outcomes I envision, pros and cons of decision + calculated risks:

What I want to invest in:

_____

Outcomes I envision:

_____

Advantages of these decisions:

_____

Disadvantages of these decisions:

_____

Risks:

_____

☐ Schedule a meeting with the leadership team with the sole agenda of the decision I want to make.

_____

☐ Outline how to meet the parameters we need to look at for a reasoned decision.

_____

☐ Collect the data, research – do the numbers.

What expertise do we need to call in?

_____

☐ Test out 2-3 case scenarios. Compare:

_____

☐ Set a time limit to make the decision and MAKE IT!

Notes on decision rationale:

_____

☐ Set up the strategies and actions to support that decision. Let's go!

Strategies and actions:

_____

CHAPTER THREE

THE INFLUENCE FACTOR

"It is so rewarding to be able to make an impact on the lives of others. It is my "why" for being put on this earth."

—**Nancy Rizzuto,** Founding Partner and
Principal of CAP STRAT

Any business leader can go through their days doing the job, making transactions, turning a profit, supporting their lifestyle. I'm going to guess that your goal is not to become just "any" business leader, because you're here with me right now.

You want more! Your Inner Visionary looks beyond the bottom line to opportunities to impact the world and add meaning to your life. You can see the future and make it happen. You inspire others to join you in making that vision a reality.

What you want to do is 10X your leadership influence.

The Influence Factor: True success in business is no longer measured just by how well you transact deals; it's how well you build relationships that inspire, motivate, and help others be their best selves.

Three keys to becoming a Visionary Influencer

KEY #1:
EXPAND YOUR INNER VISIONARY AS AN INFLUENCER.

I believe that every person we choose to connect with can be an influencer, from the C-Suite exec, the people who help keep our firms running, our customers and vendors, our networking colleagues, to the people whose paths we cross on a regular basis.

Too many leaders make the mistake of staying in their own silos with a narrow-minded view of how – and with whom – they should do business. They leave valuable and creative opportunities on the table, and miss out on meeting people who could advance their business and maybe even change their lives for the better!

Visionary Action Step #1:
[Re]Define "influencer" – those you influence
and who can influence you.

Influence for the Visionary Leader is not just about transactional relation-ships attached to dollar signs (this from a person who loves her numbers!). The thing is, you can do both. Here is what influence means to the best of the best:

- A bigger-picture vision beyond transactions toward building deep and long-lasting relationships that can, in fact, increase your sales and success.

- Connecting with people in the spirit of giving and winning (not always financially), recognizing their ability to make an impact on you or how you could make an impact on them.
- Harnessing the magic of those unplanned encounters – at your local coffee shop, discovering that an old friend is now your perfect business resource, or finding out you share a common interest with a client that leads to next-level opportunities to work with them.

The more you adopt and practice this mindset, the more possibilities and opportunities you'll see. With the influence of a variety of people who bring their unique experience, expertise, and perspective to the table, your vision continues to expand.

> *"What can help you get out of your own way is to surround yourself with smart people who can help fill in gaps, challenge, and identify things that may not be a natural comfort zone for you as a leader."*
> —**Laura Held,** *Partner at Shamrock Capital*[9]

The most exciting part, which I love about being a Visionary Influencer, is the ripple effect of influence that you never could have anticipated. This is how it has worked for me ...

The New York chapter of a nonprofit organization called Best Buddies International[10] was founded to provide one-to-one friendships, integrated employment, and leadership development programs for people with intellectual and developmental disabilities (in my influencer role I'm sharing the link to their website here (https://www.bestbuddies.org/) where you can read more about the amazing work they do – who knows what impact my gesture will have, right?).

Marilyn, a dear friend of mine, has been involved for over 20 years, and invited me to one of their fundraising galas to support the jobs program she spearheaded. The first ripple effect for me was one of the speakers, a young man with a disability who told his story of the job opportunity he got through this program. He was a phenomenal speaker, captivating the audience who gave him a resounding standing ovation. He inspired me so much that I couldn't wait to share his story with anyone who would listen – and resolved to be a better Visionary Leader myself.

Then I ran into a friend at the reception who's a successful business owner and, in his spare time, a nonprofit maven. When he found out I knew Marilyn he asked if I would introduce them, which of course I did, knowing that this connection could be a win for both. Later that evening he in turn introduced me to a contact of his – which resulted in landing me a client contract with a terrific nonprofit.

There's more! A month or so later, through a casual conversation with a colleague working with a printing association, she told me their biggest challenge was finding help in the warehouse. I said, "You're missing an entire workforce! Have you thought about nonprofit jobs programs for people who have disabilities?" We started brainstorming other opportunities such as people who've been incarcerated for minor crimes, retirees who still want to work, or opportunities for students in community college.

I offered to help the printing association research and connect to resources, including of course the Best Buddies program, and reaching out to my contacts (who were thrilled to help). The association gratefully offered to pay me for this effort but I refused, saying this was about making a difference – if we employ these people, we have a better society. I felt like the grateful one to have been able to make a meaningful impact for just a few hours of my time.

Authenticity is the critical piece here. If you decide to influence someone for the purpose of getting an immediate return, it's not going to work. It may even backfire because people can sniff out inauthenticity and manipulation – and they won't like it.

Instead, find ways to contribute that light you up, that you feel good about doing. Tap into your Inner Visionary – especially your X Factor – to unleash those qualities, talents, and interests that set you apart and will have a positive impact on someone or something. **Give freely, enjoy yourself, and stay open to the rewards that will come.**

Visionary Action Step #2:
Explore who and what influences you.

I'm sure you've been asked before: "Who are your biggest influences?" And you might answer with some well-known names of history's and society's most renown figures. That's great!

Now let's next-level the question …

Think of who the influencers are in your everyday life. If you're like most people, you have relationships in areas such as:

- Community (family, neighbors, clubs, religious organizations, etc.)
- Business associations, networking groups, alumni groups
- Current coworkers, colleagues and clients
- Former coworkers, colleagues and clients
- Charities and nonprofit associations; other volunteer activities
- Hobbies and leisure activities that bring you together with people

1. **Jot these categories down** as a prompt, and under each one start listing people who have influenced you in a positive way, no matter how large or small. Think beyond the typical. Challenge yourself to fill in 5-10 people for each category.

2. **Think about the ways** these people have influenced you, and how you might have influenced them. Consider: *What are the qualities they have that I admire or want to emulate?*

3. **Follow up!**

- Keep these people in mind to continue your connection in a meaningful way, from simply taking a moment to thank a person for the impact they had on you, to proactively reaching out to people whose relationship you want to develop more.
- Make some decisions to focus on surrounding yourself with the positive influences more often – and to start moving away from the negative ones.

Visionary Action Step #3:
Put influence into practice: mentorship

I would not be where I am today if I hadn't had great mentors. Mentorship is so important, and I want to impress upon you that **there's never a "wrong" time to seek out a mentor or to be one.** Age doesn't matter. Whether you're early in your career or later in your life, having a mentor to help guide you is crucial any time you want to make a transformational decision, try something different or go bigger.

There are many forms of mentorship, including professional mentors. I like to think of mentorship more organically as an element of the Influence Factor. Simply put, it's looking to someone who can point something out to you that you hadn't known or thought of before. Or offering that same guidance to influence someone else in a positive way. You get to define what mentoring is for yourself, and reap its beautiful rewards.

"People I've met along the way come to me wanting mentoring or to have a coffee chat to learn from me. Those same people have gone on to do some really brilliant things in their life. And they've never forgotten that I made time to give them that space. If you can make time for someone else, it will come back to you." ~Joi Gordon, cofounder of Rapport Inc. and Gordon Hewes Consulting[11]

KEY #2:
SHOW UP EVERY DAY FROM
A PLACE OF "I CARE."

Positive influence happens in the seemingly tiniest encounters that occur during the day. Compare how your morning would start if, instead of that cheerful barista who remembers your name and your coffee order, the people at the coffee shop were rude and growly and treated you every day as if you were a stranger to them. Which kind of experience would you prefer?

Even the words you were taught to say as a child – "yes, please" and "no, thank you" – are simple acts of courtesy that show we care. Yet how quickly civility can get lost in a workplace especially when you're in a deadline crunch, crisis situation, or dealing with difficult people.

Going to work each day can become a living hell for someone who feels disrespected, ignored, harassed, or not valued. Many of today's workers aren't having it. They'll transfer out of a department or leave a company to find a more positive work environment.

Tapping into the Influence Factor means recognizing this simple truth: **People want to be seen, heard, respected, and valued. You want that from others and they want it from you, especially as their leader.**

Visionary Action Step #4:
Build relationships with respectful and
meaningful communication.

*1) **Treat everyone with common courtesy*** – always, no matter who they are or why you are interacting with them. Because it's the right and respectful thing to do, of course.

And … you might have heard the expression *"you get more flies with honey than with vinegar?"* Unpleasant and mean, or polite and kind – which behavior is more likely to bring you a positive outcome? Choose how you are going to communicate with any contact regardless of how angry or annoyed you might feel, so that you get the best outcome from the encounter.

2) *Plan how you will show up* at a meeting, in a phone call, writing an email or text, etc. Instead of just jumping in, do this: Stop for a moment and think about ...

- *What is the outcome I am looking to achieve as a result of this communication/meeting?*
- *Is my communication meaningful, respectful, relevant?*
- *What influence is my communication going to have on them, and how can I leverage my message to get the best outcome for both of us?*

Be that Visionary Influencer who is going to build your relationships on respect, kindness, and caring. Build the "know, like and trust" that has people wanting to engage with you and buy from you.

Visionary Action Step #5:
Make your influence your brand.

Today's world of business is all about content. We are presenting ourselves on our website, social media, in the news, on podcasts, in live meetings and on live stages.

Take your role as business professional and influencer very seriously in terms of how you desire to be perceived by the world. Look at the big picture and the ripple effect of your brand.

- *What does my brand say about me?*
- *Where and how is the content landing on the minds and hearts of my audience?*

"I had a vision from the beginning of who I wanted to be as an attorney, and it really came down to staying open and taking steps forward. As I met people and they liked and trusted me, I just became their go-to person – suddenly I have an international practice! When you stay open, these things just organically grow."
—**Nina Marino,** *Partner at Kaplan Marino*[12]

1) *Identify and assess the content that's in line with the way you want to be seen,* and the content that is not. Make those changes where you can. There isn't much you can do to retract content that's floating in cyberspace forever, but you can start fresh with new, inspiring, motivating messaging.

"There is no such thing as bad publicity" may work for a celebrity but, in the long game, it is NOT a good business model!

Above all, be yourself. Nina Marino shared with me that when she became a lawyer entering the world of criminal defense, there were very few private practitioners like her, a young blond woman. She was an anomaly and found it hard to command respect. Yet she learned to embrace being different. "I think that being the anomaly is something that everyone should use in the best way they can – sometimes it's better to not be like everybody else."

2) *Make it personal.* Tap into your X Factor to show up as the unique influencer that you are. One November I emailed a prospect to try to get back on their calendar and opened with, "Hi, Happy Thanksgiving! I realized your son went off to college this year. You must be so excited for him to be coming home for Thanksgiving. How are things going?"

How did I remember that? Believe me, I do not have a memory like an elephant – I keep notes! When I'm ready to reach out to someone, I take a few moments to check my notes on them so I can be in touch with their business and personal lives to make a personal connection with them. It's enjoyable for me; it's part of my X Factor. And it's become one of my main marketing tools – because it works.

KEY #3:
EMBED INFLUENCE IN YOUR ORG CULTURE.

Now let's turn your Visionary Influencer outward into your organization. Here are three truths about leadership and influence:

- You hold power and responsibility by virtue of being a leader.
- People are looking to you for guidance and example.
- Whether or not you pay attention to your behavior or the encounters you have in your business, *others do.*

The Visionary Leader is going to leverage their role and responsibility by creating an environment that reflects their influence brand and the company's values, which will set the tone for everyday behavior within the organization as well as outfacing, and will show you care personally and *as a company.*

We'll be talking more about org culture later in the book; here I want to lay the foundation of who you can be personally as a leader and influencer of your company ...

Visionary Action Step #6:
Set an example for your team and train them to follow.

Lead with everyday courtesy and respectful, meaningful communication to set the example for your people through your own behavior.

1) *"Make it personal" is a good guideline inside your company* as well as for outside relationships. Every Monday I hold a team online meeting which starts with sharing highlights of everyone's weekend. Since we are not physically gathered around a conference table and have a view into everyone's home office/living room/kitchen/you-name-it, I make it a point to notice their environment. "Hey, is that the new couch you've been waiting to get delivered? It's beautiful!"

Keep these personal moments short and within boundaries that you will have already established:

- *What for you is friendly and develops a good relationship*
- *What for you goes too far and violates personal boundaries*

Once you are clear on these boundaries, make sure you enforce them with your team.

2) *Train your team to make sure all outfacing encounters reflect your influencer brand.* Modeling your own behavior is a good starting point, yet not everyone has the natural skills of communication or common courtesy.

> **The Four Seasons Hotels and Resorts have an impeccable** global reputation for customer satisfaction (and no surprise, also for employee engagement and retention, listed on *Fortune*'s "100 Best Places to Work" for 20 years). Their organizational culture and training are based on their belief that the front line is the key to a great customer experience. [13]
>
> My colleague's son took a job at the Four Seasons as a pastry chef. Even though his position in the kitchen wasn't customer-facing, he took the 12-week training program that every employee takes to learn the company's standards and expectations. Fifteen years and other jobs later, he remembers this training as one of the most influential to his professional development.
>
> You might not have to go as far as 12-week intensive training in your firm, but you get the idea. Consider what the appropriate training would look like for your particular firm that will bring everyone together and up to speed.

3) *Be visible. Be available.* Find ways to keep informal connections happening with your teams, partners and employees, especially in the shifting work environments we continue to experience.

If yours is a fully remote or hybrid workplace, you have to get creative about offering those old-school "water cooler" hangout experiences where spontaneous exchanges are still shown to build connections and spark innovative ideas. How do you make yourself visible and available to your people?

One of my client companies schedules time for their staff to engage with them with questions or comments, and are seeing great success with this. Each of the four partners takes one hour per week to open their calendars for their 70+ staff to connect with them on a meeting platform. Here's how it can work:

Schedule time a couple of hours a week, say Tuesdays and Thursdays, 12:00 to 1:00. You open your online meeting platform on that regular basis to anyone, and be there for people to pop in with a question, check-in, or have a conversation.

If no one shows up, great – you have the hour to catch up on your work. If people do show up, there can be a lot of value in that exchange:

- Just for your people to know you are offering a point of contact makes a positive impact.
- A quick question posed to you becomes a spontaneous, brilliant conversation.
- An emerging star may rise whose professional development you can mentor.
- You see the kinds of questions people are asking, and can solicit their opinions and feedback to improve the company.
- Other leaders may take your lead and create their own version of open office hours.
- More creative connections may be spawned like an online coffee break or book club. Connections being made; meaningful relationships being built!

The Influence Factor:
TAKEAWAYS

Success in business is measured by how well you build relationships that inspire, motivate, and help others be their best selves.

- Expand your vision of what an influencer "looks" like beyond the conventional and in your everyday life.
- Discover and define what and who are positive influences on you, and surround yourself with those people and input.
- Put the Influence Factor into practice by mentoring and being mentored.

Show up every day from a place of "I care," through simple acts of courtesy and personal attention – and you'll attract positive responses and desired outcomes.

- Be a positive influence with your workforce and other business contacts.
- Build relationships with respectful and meaningful communication.
- Make influence your personal and professional brand.

Embed influence in your organizational culture, in a positive, pro-active, and purposeful way.

- Set an example for your team and train them to follow; maintain good boundaries.
- "Make it personal" is a good guideline for your behavior inside the company and out.
- Be visible, be available to your people to keep informal connections happening adapted to a remote or hybrid environment.

INFLUENCERS IN MY LIFE WORKSHEET

INSTRUCTIONS:

1. Think of who the influencers are in your everyday life, in each of the categories below.
2. List 5-10 people in each category who have influenced you in a positive way.
3. Jot down 1-3 words that describe the qualities you admire or want to emulate.
4. Follow up! Draft a plan on how you can continue your connection with these people in a meaningful way.
   - Community (family, neighbors, clubs, religious organizations, etc.)

1. _____ : _____ , _____ , _____

2. _____ : _____ , _____ , _____

3. _____ : _____ , _____ , _____

4. _____ : _____ , _____ , _____

5. _____ : _____ , _____ , _____

6. _____ : _____ , _____ , _____

7. _____ : _____ , _____ , _____

8. _____ : _____ , _____ , _____

9. _____ : _____ , _____ , _____

10. _____ : _____ , _____ , _____

- Business associations, networking groups, alumni groups

1. _____ : _____ , _____ , _____

2. _____ : _____ , _____ , _____

3. _____ : _____ , _____ , _____

4. _____ : _____ , _____ , _____

5. _____ : _____ , _____ , _____

6. _____ : _____ , _____ , _____

7. _____ : _____ , _____ , _____

8. _____ : _____ , _____ , _____

9. _____ : _____ , _____ , _____

10. _____ : _____ , _____ , _____

- Current coworkers, colleagues, and clients

1. _____ : _____ , _____ , _____

2. _____ : _____ , _____ , _____

3. _____ : _____ , _____ , _____

4. _____ : _____ , _____ , _____

5. _____ : _____ , _____ , _____

6. _____ : _____ , _____ , _____

7. _____ : _____ , _____ , _____

8. _____ : _____ , _____ , _____

9. _____ : _____ , _____ , _____

10. _____ : _____ , _____ , _____

- Former colleagues and clients

1. _____ : _____ , _____ , _____

2. _____ : _____ , _____ , _____

3. _____ : _____ , _____ , _____

4. _____ : _____ , _____ , _____

5. _____ : _____ , _____ , _____

6. _____ : _____ , _____ , _____

7. _____ : _____ , _____ , _____

8. _____ : _____ , _____ , _____

9. _____ : _____ , _____ , _____

10. _____ : _____ , _____ , _____

- Charities and nonprofit associations; other volunteer activities

1. _____ : _____ , _____ , _____

2. _____ : _____ , _____ , _____

3. _____ : _____ , _____ , _____

4. _____ : _____ , _____ , _____

5. _____ : _____ , _____ , _____

6. _____ : _____ , _____ , _____

7. _____ : _____ , _____ , _____

8. _____ : _____ , _____ , _____

9. _____ : _____ , _____ , _____

10. _____ : _____ , _____ , _____

- Hobbies and leisure activities that bring you together with people

1. _____ : _____ , _____ , _____

2. _____ : _____ , _____ , _____

3. _____ : _____ , _____ , _____

4. _____ : _____ , _____ , _____

5. _____ : _____ , _____ , _____

6. _____ : _____ , _____ , _____

7. _____ : _____ , _____ , _____

8. _____ : _____ , _____ , _____

9. _____ : _____ , _____ , _____

10. _____ : _____ , _____ , _____

Follow-up Plan:

How can you continue your connection with these people in a meaningful way?

_____

_____

_____

_____

CHAPTER FOUR

GAINING 17X CONFIDENCE

"Entrepreneurship is a fast-track course in personal development, and self-confidence is at the top of the syllabus."

—**Ivy Slater,** Slater Success

In Chapter One we talked about "personal power" – not the position you hold, but the attitude of confidence, strength, and self-mastery you embody. Personal power spotlights your X Factor, expands your influence, sparks and sustains your momentum, and boosts your ability to face unforeseen obstacles.

Confidence is an inner self-knowledge and self-assurance that inspires and drives everything you do. Confidence makes you that person other people are drawn to, and can create a major impact on the world.

Heady stuff, right? It's the kind of Visionary Leader you want to be, but … maybe you are also thinking (hedging, hesitating, doubting) about how this could possibly be obtainable. *Could I ever be this person?*

I have some answers – let's start with a question: *Did you forget about when you were a kid?*

The No. 1 thing to know about 17X-ing your confidence

Remember the games you played as a kid? There were Follow the Leader, Hide and Seek, Capture the Flag, Red Light Green Light, Kickball, and all the ones you and your friends made up on your own.

How many times did you get to be a captain or leader? When were you the one who got to make the decisions, create the plan, be in charge, lead the team? As a kid, you took on these roles with confidence! You believed in your abilities without question. You delegated tasks to the other kids on the team, knowing their strengths. You encouraged everyone. You set goals. You were proud of what you accomplished at the end of it.

You didn't *think* about confidence; you just *were* confident.

What happened to that confident kid?

Why, as an adult, does the concept of confident leadership become a lot scarier? When and why do we lose confidence in ourselves and our ability to lead? It can stem from a variety of life circumstances. But I'm here to tell you that this brave kid, the one who took charge and led the game, dreamt BIG dreams, had that feeling of endless possibility – ***that confident kid still lives inside of you.***

YOU'VE BEEN THAT CONFIDENT LEADER ALL ALONG.

In my work with business leaders, we focus on revenue and growth, yes, but we also focus on the inner work. Not to say that I invariably lead a client call with, "Hey, let's meet today on your personal development!" but you and I both know that the inner game is at least as important as the outer game for true success. People love to work with me because I have the ability and instincts (and guts) to tackle both, and in the course of any given session the inner game may come up and personal breakthroughs happen.

It may surprise you to know that what comes up most often for clients is *lack of confidence*. This is why I chose to highlight this topic.

Exec-level professionals have a certain amount of confidence or else they wouldn't be where they are today. You can say with confidence: *I'm a professional. I'm capable. I have reached a level of success that I can be proud of.*

Yet, there comes a point at which even great leaders face a confidence crisis. You want to continue to grow your company and yourself. So, you are constantly stretching into something uncomfortable because you haven't done it before. The 5 million-dollar business that you want to grow to $20 million; your firm of forty people you want to scale to 150; your vision of launching offices in Europe and Asia in the next two years.

Something blocks you from taking that next step you know you need to take for next-level growth. There is some area where you don't quite believe enough in your abilities. Or it might show up as full-fledged Impostor Syndrome where you feel like a fraud. I've seen this experience in some of the most successful leaders I've ever known. In fact, it's often the highest-achievers who have the most difficulty accepting their successes because the bar they've held for themselves is sometimes too high to reach.

I want you to know that these "blocks" are a natural part of getting to the best of the best. When you recognize it's happening to you, you are then empowered to do something about it.

So, how do you ...

- Recognize that there's something blocking that confidence you know is inside you?
- Shift that mindset to the next big vision or the next best version of yourself?
- Turn that mindset into actions that will get you the results you want?

In other words, how do you become the full-speed-ahead Visionary Leader that the younger version of yourself would be so proud of?

Start right here ...

Visionary Action Step #1:
The Top 10 Things Technique.

Today, maybe even right now, take a moment to reflect back on ALL the amazing things you have done in your life, both personally and professionally.

You have overcome obstacles and challenges. You have figured things out when you never thought you could. You have found ways to manage unexpected economic downturns, history-changing global events – even disasters (natural and otherwise) which you never dreamed would be part of your life. And you are here today, still standing strong and facing tomorrow.

1. ***Choose your top ten*** from all those amazing things you can think of, and write them down in some format you can refer to again and often. Many people like to have a journal where they keep notes, thoughts, and actions (like you're finding in this book) on personal and leadership development. I encourage my clients to keep a "success journal" on a regular basis.

    This is not just teenage-diary fluff – according to brain science, when you physically write down thoughts and ideas, you activate your brain to embed them in your memory.[14] I start every client call by asking them to share a success. It is so easy to find fault with ourselves and to self-criticize, that it's important to stop and recognize you and your achievement.

2. ***Be honest with yourself – don't sugarcoat or gloss over your successes.*** Write down everything you can about each incident, like:

    - *What was the measurable outcome of the project I headed?*
    - *Whose mind did I change that turned things around for the better?*
    - *What was the result of facing that obstacle or clearing that road-block in a process?*
    - *What was the dollar amount of the sales month I had that won me the top performer award?*

3. ***Keep this information so you can refer back to these ten things*** whenever you feel doubt about your abilities or drop into Impostor Syndrome. Read them aloud with energy and intent (another way to embed thoughts and beliefs in your brain). Celebrate them often!

Being reminded of your successes will shift your mindset and build confidence for the action you are about to take. Here is an example of how it worked for one person in real time:

Ivy's Office Hours: As we gathered in the main hall to kick off a client retreat I was giving, each person stood up and introduced themselves to the group – who they were and what they did. Everyone knew I would be offering on-the-spot coaching, and it wasn't long before I was already jumping in.

One attendee introduced herself as Caroline, told us her title and then launched into what felt to me like someone else's script, using long words, formal statements and jargon to describe her work. Then she quickly sat down. It was clear that her words did not reflect her; in fact, they probably didn't make sense to anyone outside her profession. She was NOT owning her work with confidence.

Me: *Thank you, Caroline. Would you mind standing up and giving us your introduction again? And this time try to be a little more direct about what it is you do for your clients.*

She stood again and repeated the exact same thing verbatim. I addressed the group:

Does everybody understand what Caroline's work is? Would you please raise your hand if you do? Not a hand went up.

Me: *Caroline, I'm sure there are people in this room who would love to work with you. But they are not getting a sense of how you could help them from what you're telling us. So, let's go about this a different way. Have you gotten a great result or had a successful meeting with a client this last month?* She nodded. Great! *Tell us about it – What happened, and how did it turn out?*

Hesitant at first, Caroline started to tell the story. It wasn't long before she began to talk with enthusiasm and even showed us some humor, which was delightful. I could feel the whole room relax.

I continued, asking questions about other customers who like to work with her, what her strengths were, and what results she gets – all designed to help her get to the essence of what she does and how she makes a difference for the people who hire her.

Suddenly she lit up – she got it! It was like her confidence level, well, 17X-ed!

Caroline had been hiding behind other people's words to describe herself because she didn't believe in her own words. Everything opened up in her and her introduction was amazing. I asked the group, *Did you get that?*

In response everyone stood up and applauded – I think we all knew what had just happened here, and it was beautiful.

Let me tell you, I see this happening in some of my most brilliant and savvy clients. Especially when it comes to speaking about themselves (aka selling), all those confidence killers can pop up at any moment. Pinning Caroline down (gently) to naming the essence of her gifts and value, bringing her work to life, and spotlighting her strengths made a lasting difference in her self-awareness and confidence.

This is what I want for you. And I know you'll see a difference in the response – and success – you receive.

Three keys to building baseline confidence for visionary action

Buoyed with your list of the amazing things you've accomplished, let's work with your Inner Visionary so you can put your confidence into action.

KEY # 1:
GO BOLDLY BECAUSE YOU KNOW WHERE YOU'RE HEADED.

A large part of confidence is knowing not only who you are, but also where you're going and why. Here is a blueprint to help (by the way, it's never too late to start!).

Visionary Action Step #2:
Follow the Alignment Process to determine
the direction you're heading.

The Alignment Process is for your personal life, exactly where you are right now and what you want to do and have in the future. We start with the end you want to see, and then work backward to what you need to do to get there. Use the worksheet at the end of this chapter as a guide.

1. *Answer this: What would I like my next [6 or 12] months to look like?* The prompts below will help. Feel free to add your own that resonate (for example, I personally love to travel so I always include the travel question – that might not be your thing):

    - *What makes me happy? What do I like to do that inspires and satisfies me?*
    - *What are important events coming up? Think of things like a milestone birthday, major graduation, wedding, grandchildren, upcoming move.*

- *Do I want to travel anywhere in the next 6-12 months? If so, where would I like to go?*
- *What do I want to splurge on at this time of my life?*

Get it all down – if it has you feeling jazzed you're on the right track!

2. **Explore this: How can my company/business complement this vision?** What do I need to do to get there?

Get creative as you look for the alignments between your vision and what your business needs/plans are, or could be.

Ivy's Office Hours (for herself): For decades I've taken myself through the Alignment Process each Q4 to update my last plan and set up the following year or so. Here's an example of my process:

I want to go to Morocco and London within the next five years, plus at least two must-do visits with family every year. So, I do the numbers ....

Let's say I estimate all my travel costs will be $100,000 a year. This year I have a plan to expand my business through more visibility, and a major aspect is to do paid keynotes globally.

What alignment can I find here? What if I focus on looking for speaking gigs that will pay for some of the travel through fees and/or covering my expenses? What if I look for engagements in locations where I want to visit? What if I stayed and worked in London for a while as a launchpad for those European speaking and personal trips?

I also want to be on the West Coast more to visit friends and family. What if I used this as an opportunity to expand my business there by focusing on landing speaking engagements and potential client meetings in the area?

Next step: Let's play out the scenarios in terms of the numbers. What income would I have to make in London to support that plan? How many paid speaking or training gigs would cover my personal visits?

All of a sudden, I'm not paying for my trip out of "retirement funds." I'm funding it out of current earnings and business deductions *while* expanding my client base!

Now I plan out where I'm headed in the next several months. I have the foundation to make confident, solid decisions on next steps, and I'll tweak or pivot as needed along the way. For example:

- Focus on a new region to expand my business for greater profit.
- Have my assistant investigate speaking opportunities in the locations I want.
- Set up my systems to support extended virtual work.

At regular intervals I take my clients through the Alignment Process, and over the years it's been extremely satisfying to see what incredible results they are making happen, both in their business and personal lives. The two really can work together for greater, holistic success!

KEY # 2:
SURROUND YOURSELF WITH PEOPLE WHO BELIEVE IN YOU.

One of the hardest things to do is to teach ourselves to believe in ourselves enough to take fearless action. Figuring it out on your own isn't easy. Thankfully, we don't have to.

> *"It's inconceivable to think that you always have to know all the answers and be able to act on them! Don't be afraid to ask for help, no matter how senior a person you are."*
> —**Beth Dahle,** *Cofounder at Impact 100 Philadelphia*[15]

An important part of confidence development is to have **somebody who will stand with you and for you.** Someone who can see more than you can see yourself. Someone you know you can trust, who'll be honest with you without a personal agenda, and who can help you believe in your ability to go boldly with confidence.

You might have heard U.S. presidents talking about their "kitchen cabinet." It's an informal circle of advisers who have a close personal, trusted relationship with the president. With all the pressures a global leader faces, you can only imagine how important this group would be to help keep their confidence up and perspective clear.

When you're faced with big decisions and your confidence gets challenged and self-doubt takes over, wouldn't it be great to know that you had people like that to turn to? An exponential confidence multiplier!

**Visionary Action Step #3:
Find your own "kitchen cabinet," people who
believe in you, will stand by you, and see in you
the vision you want for yourself.**

Each person and business has their own set of unique challenges and struggles. The support you build for yourself is also going to be unique to you; it's yours to decide what you need.

1) Ask: What kind of support do I want? *What kind of person will be the "right" one to trust and hold my vision with me?* Be open but focused – as much as you love your best friend, this may not be a role they're able to fill. Your COO might not be someone you feel like going out for a beer with, but they completely "get" you and your vision, and you trust them implicitly.

2) Tap into these sources: your close friends, frat/sorority alum, mentors, coaches, organizations or networking groups you're involved in. Or choose new connections that will match your "new" vision of where you want to be.

3) ***The key to your own kitchen cabinet is to see it and own it*** – because you need it, you deserve it, and it's critical to your success.

"Putting a good team around you is so important – not only for the success of your business, but also for the success of your personal life." ~Stacy Francis, President and CEO of Francis Financial[16]

KEY #3:
OUTSIDE YOUR COMFORT ZONE?
DO IT ANYWAY – FOR YOURSELF AND
FOR YOUR BUSINESS.

The amazing things you've done (and are) got you to where you are today. The question now becomes: *Do you want to stay where you are today, or do you want to expand, grow and scale your business?*

I hope your answer is to expand, *grow and scale!*

Sitting in your comfort zone does not grow a business or a life. Period.

> *"Even as devastating as some of my setbacks were, I could look back and connect the dots to where I was today and say, oh, my gosh, it was because of that failure that I made this decision, which helped me get to the next role."*
> —**Peter Ruppert,** *the late CEO at Fusion Education Group*[17]

As we know, the most successful entrepreneurs are people who will not shy away from risk taking. Is it scary for them? Sure. Deciding to go skydiving doesn't mean you're not scared out of your mind.

My son was planning to go skydiving during a trip to New Zealand. He was only 17 so I had to sign the release (which might have been the scariest thing *I've* ever done!). When the day came, I literally waited by the phone for his call to tell me he had landed safely. Which, of course, he did.

The phone finally rings, I pick up, and hear his voice, *Hi Mom, I'm fine.*

After an enormous sigh of relief, I respond as nonchalantly as I can, *Great! Well, how was it?*

Mom, Truth? I was scared shitless ... And it was the best thing I've ever done in my life. It was the most exhilarating, fantastic thing I've ever done! I'm so glad I didn't back out.

Visionary Action Step #4:
Take incremental steps into the next best version of you as a confident leader.

Of course, we don't have to skydive to prove our confidence. But every day gives you the chance to build your confidence little by little by thinking about something new, working on your vision, or taking small steps toward accomplishing whatever goals you've committed to.

You may not have full inner confidence or full belief in any of it just yet – *and you don't have to.* It's about the small steps that take you out of your comfort zone and the calculated risks you take day by day.

Belief and confidence build together with every step you take toward your vision.

You slay the first tiny dragon, then a bigger one, and a bigger one. You celebrate each step and obstacle you overcome even if you didn't defeat all the dragons out there.

You begin to see results, whether it's bigger numbers, more hires, introducing new products to the market, an invitation to acquire or be acquired ... and

you realize that you're settling into a new norm of the new you. You BECOME that Visionary Leader who just 2Xed, 5Xed, 17Xed their confidence.

You probably know what I'm talking about, as you've likely been there already, haven't you? If so, keep at it! As you go forward, be sure to stop and notice those moments when they happen – celebrate them and remember them to tap into the next time you decide to go for something even bigger and scarier.

Visionary Action Step #5:
Take an action outside your comfort zone
and run with it.

My company started doing LinkedIn Live shows as part of the increased visibility plan that came out of the Alignment Process I did. In the first year we hosted more than 30 shows, bringing in guests from various organizations to share their expertise and answer viewer questions live.

Taking this step was very scary for me – going live and tackling the whole tech part of producing these on a regular basis were things I'd never done before. While I'm a big fan of tech, the truth is it can intimidate me. And as much as I love speaking in front of any number of people, it was different going live online, managing the conversations with the guests and fielding questions from the viewers while handling third-party streaming services and internet issues.

But it has been so worth it – and easier as we go along. I'm honing my interview and speaking skills, because there is no better training than thinking on your feet in a live event. My guests were amazing, and we built many long-term connections through this avenue. My company has expanded our brand and our reach, while showcasing our guests to expand theirs.

As a result of this visibility, within four weeks I received seven speaking engagements and got a new client from my podcast.

Taking this first big step has 10Xed my confidence and momentum, and is seeding and accelerating other plans for expanding into more podcasts, online roundtables, and next-level paid speaking gigs.

While at first this whole idea felt like skydiving without a parachute, now it's part of my professional and personal brand. One step at a time ...

Do a project that scares you a little and remember to:

- Face the fear.
- Go all-in with it – don't skimp or go halfway, that's the worst form of self-sabotage. This means getting the resources and team you need to do it right.
- Be prepared to go through the learning curve, which will include mistakes and pivots.
- If it's working, keep it up and make it even better!
- Only "cut bait" (and do it fast to reduce your losses) if you find out that the project is not going to accomplish what you set out to do – which you will only have known from trying it in the first place.
- Reap the rewards and leverage the opportunities you gained from this experience.

Gaining 17X Confidence: TAKEAWAYS

No matter how successful you may be, it's common to experience times of serious self-doubt and low confidence – usually when you are poised to take a next big step.

- Remember the fearless, confident kid inside – that kid is still there to call up anytime!
- Do the Top 10 Things Technique, and use it to remind you, when you're about to take some confidence-shaking action, of those amazing things you've done, obstacles you've overcome, and successes you've had.

Work on your Inner Visionary to put your confidence into action.

- You will have more confidence to go forward if you know where you're going. Get specific.
- Take yourself through the Alignment Process to explore and list out what you want in your personal life for the next 6 - 12 months.
- Explore how your business can complement your vision. Get creative.

Surround yourself with people who believe in you, will stand by you and for you.

- Develop your own version of a "kitchen cabinet" – an informal circle of advisors you can trust to hold your vision for you, provide objective feedback, help you keep your perspective clear, and lift you up in times of self-doubts and shaken confidence.
- Find the right people to fill this role and tap into their support – you need it, you deserve it, and it's critical to your success.

Sitting in your comfort zone does not grow a business.

- If there's something you know you need to do and it's outside your comfort zone – even scary – do it anyway.
- Take incremental steps into the next version of you as a confident leader, continuing to build confidence as you accomplish more successes.
- Start now by doing a project that's outside your comfort zone and run with it. Set your goals, do your homework, get your resources, and go all in – then reap the rewards, opportunities and lessons from the experience!

ALIGNMENT PROCESS WORKSHEET

INSTRUCTIONS: The Alignment Process is to explore exactly where you are now in your personal life, and what you want to do and have in the future. Answer these questions following the prompts below: What would I like my next [6 or 12] months to look like?

1. What makes me happy? What do I like to do that inspires and satisfies me?

_____

_____

_____

2. What are important events coming up? Think of things like a milestone birthday, major graduation, wedding, grandchildren, or upcoming move.

_____

_____

_____

3. Do I want to travel anywhere in the next 6-12 months? If so, where would I like to go?

_____

_____

_____

4. What do I want to splurge on at this time of my life?

_____

_____

_____

5. Your question here:

_____

_____

_____

6. Your question here:

_____

_____

_____

7. Your question here:

_____

_____

_____

CHAPTER FIVE

BUILDING MULTIMILLION DOLLAR MAGIC

"The sweet spot – the balance – is slowing down and seeing what sticks, because it's easy to zig and zag on the various ideas and opportunities that come your way."

—**Larry Perkins,** Founder and CEO of SierraConstellation Partners, management consulting and advisory[18]

We've talked about staying on top of your numbers, expanding your Inner Visionary as an influencer, and beginning to take actions that will create the business you envision. Now let's go deeper into how you're going to make your numbers work for your business – and for your life.

Martin, CEO of a national digital marketing company, came to me with a big growth vision and revenues of about $900,000. Martin is a delightful, ambitious guy who loves what he's doing for clients – and for years had been consistently undercharging them for the value their firm was bringing.

The first year of our work together was mainly a series of mindset push-pull exercises to help Martin believe in the level of service they offer and to align it with their pricing. I showed them how doing their numbers justified raising their rates, and we worked together on ways they could make the client conversions they dreamed of.

Within a few months they got their first $120,000 client. That opened the floodgates for Martin – *We can do this!* Within a few quarters of a concerted marketing effort and some key hires, they were able to push their numbers above the million-dollar level and continue steady and solid seven-figure growth.

Law firm founding partners Madeline and George had exceeded their numbers last year, and their first decision was to pay their partners and top associates more. While I certainly wasn't against raising salaries, I knew that before pulling a multimillion-dollar trigger like that, some analyses and number-crunching needed to be done first. I went into question mode with them to identify:

- *Was last year a fluke or is it something sustainable?*
- *What amount do you want your partners to make next year?*
- *What will it cost to add much-needed capacity so your firm can scale even more?*
- *Have you looked at the number of contingency cases you've taken in the last two years? How many hourly?*
- *What effect does this percentage have on your numbers and/ or cash flow?*
- *Which cases netted the most money?*
- *What did the best cases look like?*

From this big-picture holistic analysis, we established financial goals for the firm based on expanding their client base to raise salaries *while investing in growth.*

The firm made the wise decisions to give a more modest raise to the partners, add capacity by hiring more staff, and focus their energy on the cases that were most lucrative and which formed a balanced client base of hourly and contingency work. They now have a solid footing that continues to see higher profits year over year.

The common thread in these two success stories is that these companies were sitting on goldmines they couldn't see, so they were making small, short-sighted decisions that were keeping them stuck in status quo numbers.

My "magic" was to offer some outside perspective and experience, to open their eyes to the opportunities in front of them, and to help them read their numbers story – which they were able to turn into revenue gold.

In this chapter I'm going to share with you how it's done so you can close more sales and make some multimillion-dollar magic for yourself!

What multimillion dollar magic is NOT

If you want me to tell you – like many business books and coaches out there – that I can promise a way for you to hit seven figures in seven months or double your monthly income within one quarter, then you might want to skip this chapter and move on ...

Mind you, these things can be done (I have clients who've made huge, rapid leaps); however, that's not the norm. What you usually find out is that (like Madeline and George did) they're not actually making that kind of money over time.

Many factors contribute to growing and scaling, all of which need to work together to *build up to and sustain multimillion dollar levels.*

There's no magic bullet here (but then, you already knew there never is). The "magic" is in **identifying and committing to a specific set of actions you do without fail** which will build and build to the numbers you dream of reaching. It may sound simple, yet I can tell you that I have a thriving business mainly because so many people are missing (or dismissing, avoiding, resisting, afraid of, unable to commit to) the consistent actions that can take them to the rapid growth they envision and deserve.

Here is the "magic:" keeping these three secrets afloat and swimming forward together. It CAN be done, I can promise you that!

- Secret #1: Personal meaning means financial success.

- Secret #2: Lead with an unstoppable strategy.
- Secret #3: Tap into your resources and use them consistently, confidently, regularly.

Three secrets to build multimillion dollar magic

SECRET #1:
PERSONAL MEANING MEANS FINANCIAL SUCCESS.

Here is a truth: If you're running your company without a meaning that's important to you personally, you will not sustain the motivation and energy to follow through enough to achieve sustainable multimillion dollar revenue.

Look at any super successful leader and you'll see that at the core of it all, their purpose is what has given them the stamina and passion to achieve success. Whether that purpose is eradicating world hunger, building a trust for your children (or future children), or serving a need that you are uniquely qualified to provide – whatever it is, it's the thing that keeps you going, caring and happy.

It starts with what I call a **Big Bold Vision** (the exciting thing that emerges from tapping into your Inner Visionary and doing the Alignment Process). We'll go deeper into creating yours in Chapter Nine.

When you create this big, bold vision, you have to believe it can happen – with everything you've got! You have so much confidence in it that you don't give yourself any excuse NOT to be in action.

Visionary Action Step # 1:
Reject any excuses that keep you from moving forward on your Big Bold Vision.

Do not wait for the "how" because if you do, the multimillion-dollar magic will never happen. If you wait to know how it's all going to happen, you'll find yourself just treading water looking for your vision across an ocean with no horizon in sight.

Instead, even though you won't have all the answers, take action steps that will move you forward steadily. New answers and solutions will appear for the next best step, then the next, and so on.

Ivy's Office Hours: Amelia is an attorney who has a Big Bold Vision:

I care deeply about social justice and I want to change the way things are in the legal system.

I want to take care of my family.

I want to leave my legacy, so I want a succession plan in place for my law firm.

We talked about the outer parameters, the biggest possibilities she could imagine around this vision. She was stretching herself to see how far she could take it.

I asked: *How can you make it extraordinary? Can you envision ten million in three years?*

Amelia: *No, I don't think so. I'm not sure how to do that.*

Me: *OK. Let's sort through some numbers. Here is the annual revenue you're bringing in currently. And let's say your annual revenue is cover-ing the expenses* [I was scribbling numbers at this point], *so you create another 500K in each of the next three years. How would you invest it? What would that look like?*

Amelia: *I can see that possibility. But our overhead has been creeping up, and we need to work on our website to improve conversion.*

We talked about some options of covering those expenses by adjusting some actions over the next few quarters. Then we brainstormed where their greatest revenue comes from. And things started to look feasible.

Me: *So, you have these untouched areas you could be pursuing that have the potential to get you near the 500K-per-year set-aside. Now, what would it look like doubling your business without working more? What could we do to make that happen?*

We calibrated how to hire an associate, redo their website, and how many client dollars would reach our $500K set-aside goals within the next five quarters.

Amelia: *I see it! This really looks like a doable plan that will meet my vision. Like, I might even get a real vacation next year!*

SECRET #2:
LEAD WITH AN UNSTOPPABLE STRATEGY.

There comes a time in a business to stop planning from notes on a napkin, so to speak. Making multimillion dollar magic IS that time. The strategies you have been doing have gotten you this far – kudos for that! – and you're reading this book because you see something bigger and better for your business legacy.

If you are serious and all-in on your vision, then you need the models and SOPs to match it. An unstoppable strategy starts with a specific game plan to take you there.

Make the Business Growth Game Plan that will score you millions

Your game plan is the foundation of strategy forming, decision making, and progress benchmarking. I'll be honest with you – I receive pushback from some clients who claim they already have a plan and don't want to waste resources on "making another one." They will resist because the economy or business environment seems so unpredictable – why try to predict the unpredictable?

I tell them, *if you want to be the best of the best ... make a business plan for the future!* In fact, it's even more important to have a good, up-to-date game plan in your pocket when the unexpected does happens. Ask just about any company that had to navigate the 2020 global pandemic.

> *"When the 2020 pandemic hit, my business kept strong mainly because of decisions we had made earlier to keep in front of trends and focus on opportunities to build a more robust and diverse practice."*
> —**Corey S. Kupfer,** *Founder and Managing Partner at Kupfer, PLLC*[9]

A solid game plan can prepare you for any left hooks the world may throw your way. Most importantly (as you can see from my client success stories) it can guide your business to a higher level than you had even imagined possible.

Bring in your leadership or exec team to work on this together. The process itself can be game-changing and your collective results will be powerful, because the Business Growth Game Plan process:

- Forces you to look at your business holistically and get really clear on your objectives.

- Roots you in reality and often some harsh truths – sometimes real fast – but then you know exactly what you're working with.
- Brings your leadership team together as co-creators of your company's legacy, and a strong force for promoting and implementing the plan effectively.
- Expands your thinking to find new and different solutions.

From the springboard of your Business Growth Game Plan, you then do the numbers, design strategies, and take the actions to create something bigger and better.

Visionary Action Step # 2:
Plan your capacity for growth.

In my example with Madeline and George, they saw only the short view of feeding their unexpected profit directly into paychecks. They didn't have a clear idea of *how* they exceeded their goals that year.

What if their "good year" had been a one-time blip? Well, they could have had a terrible year following – and the money would have been gone while unreasonable salary expectations would have remained (which are very difficult to back out of once you've set those expectations). By looking at several scenarios and doing the numbers to map out what was possible, they were able to accomplish several of their objectives.

As you develop your game plan, always, always look to the future to what portion of your revenue you can invest to create that future – remember: Run your business from where you are going, not where you are. Think out the implications and consequences of each money decision you make. Consider all the pieces of the jigsaw puzzle and how they affect each other to create a full picture of your company on its way to meet its multilimillion dollar future.

What will set you apart from so many other firms is this tip: ***Visit your game plan often.*** It's a living, breathing work in progress that will shift and change and grow as your millions do.

Depending on the size and structure of your business, you might work with your plan in regularly scheduled staff meetings, leadership team meetings, or perhaps through a cross-functional special team that meets quarterly and reports to leadership. Set up the process of working with your Business Growth Game Plan so it becomes a routine part of your business model.

Look at your plan, do the numbers, make sound decisions, implement. And then …

Visionary Action Step # 3:
Dare to make brilliant course corrections.

Because you can't predict which doors are going to close on you, or which new doors are going to open, you want to:

- Create a plan whose core is sound and constant.
- Commit fully to the actions you decide to make.
- Assess, measure, assess, measure along the way.
- Be willing to adjust the plan.

Once you start implementing, you're going to receive new information; for example, the market research intel on the new type of clients you're looking to reach. What your target's looking for or what they want to pay may be different than you had first assessed. Good news: then you want to raise your prices or accelerate your marketing efforts. Less-good news: you'd better go back to the drawing board before making any further investment in a target that's not going to bring viable ROI.

Put a system in place to work with this information in a timely manner to answer: ***what's working, what is not, what can be done a different way.***

SECRET #3:
TAP INTO YOUR RESOURCES AND USE THEM CONSISTENTLY, CONFIDENTLY, REGULARLY.

I don't have to tell you that you could never have gotten where you are today without the processes and people you've depended on – your re-sources. Most of us, including me, tend to take for granted their value. But I've learned that this can be a big mistake, a surefire way to stifle growth and keep a business stagnant.

The secret is to **tap into your valuable resources in an intentional, systematic way,** built into your game plan, into your org culture, and into your quarterly and daily schedules.

Match your operational processes and systems with your growth goals

If you want next-level growth, you're going to want to "next-level" the pro-cesses and systems that are going to execute the three secrets of multi-million dollar magic.

> *"What got you here won't get you there. Sometimes the team doesn't have the experience or expertise internally to know what to do next or to know how to get to the next level. Sometimes you don't yet have the processes or systems that will augment their capabilities."*
> **—Laura Held,** *Partner at Shamrock Capital*[20]

When you initially built the daily operations of your business, you were in a completely different space than you are today. They most certainly need a tune-up in order to meet where you are *growing to be* in the future.

Here are the main process areas that every business needs:

- Customer care and service
- Finance - yes, the numbers of course!
- Human resources
- Internal operations
- Sales and marketing

Plan for the growth you are anticipating by paying attention to all of these areas. Some may be fine for now, others will require a tweak or two, and some may need new and dedicated resources and systems. Consider what you need early on, so you aren't blindsided by inadequacies.

When Leonard, my financial advisor client, made the decision to expand his firm's office with new space and new hires, they focused on the space and forgot to put into place the systems that were going to facilitate the recruiting, hiring, onboarding and training processes. They got caught flat-footed for sure! We had to step in and get those functions outsourced immediately.

There are always better, faster and more efficient ways to meet your future growth needs. Find them and use them.

When you're adding, revising, updating systems, *use the strengths and knowledge of your team members and trusted professionals for ideas.* No hiding in silos! I turn to my systems people when it's time to update an email provider, review web hosting, change an automation process, compare CRM systems, etc. They spend time in these systems, so they know what is working and what is not.

> *"Let your people be creative on their own and work in a way that is most applicable to them. Decide what you want to control, what you want the result to be. Then let your team get from A to B to the result."*
> —**Susan L. Combs,** *CEO of Combs & Company, LLC, and Founder of Pancakes for Roger, Inc., a Veterans non-profit.*[21]

Don't forget the processes that aren't tech- or production-related, especially if your business is in the professional services space where the core "products" are you and your people. They need and deserve organizational processes that will support them to be their best.

Consider, for instance, assessing your communication systems to make sure everyone is well informed and equipped to do their jobs, as well as active participants in the company mission and vision. Especially as the company brings on more and more people, effective communication becomes crucial.

An example of supporting your people is scheduling – at least it is for Slater Success as a services company where our client engagement is deep, frequent and complex; I travel a lot for clients, speaking and presentations, and my team works remotely.

We have calendar processes in place to make sure:

- No client contact is falling through the cracks. Ever.
- My team has regularly scheduled meetings to count on.
- Our personal needs are built into the schedule to keep us refreshed (and sane ...). For example, I try to schedule Fridays off for myself during the three months of summer, with exceptions built in for when we need to plug in a call or a podcast recording.

Think about what you can be updating, what needs changed, what needs removed, what needs added, and **who the right people are to assist in those decisions.**

Visionary Action Step 4:
Match your Standard Operating Procedures (SOPs) to your new processes and systems.

SOPs are written instructions that describe the activities necessary to complete the tasks according to your standards of running your business.

Even if you have a small company, getting operations, guidelines, and policies in writing is important to be clear and specific about what needs to get done and what your organization's expectations are. Here are just some of the reasons why it's worth the effort:

- Structure helps keep everyone on the same page – expectations are clear, we know how to do our jobs, and we know where we stand in the company at any time.
- Hiring, training and cross-functioning are much easier and less time consuming. Job descriptions and onboarding are clear. No one leaves a job taking crucial institutional memory with them. Discrimination suits or separation conflicts are reduced or eliminated.
- Customer service is standardized and on brand. *Does everyone from top to bottom know what to do if there's a complaint (or a compliment) from a customer? Does the sales team have the same communication style and service style as the marketing team?* Everyone's out-facing relationship with clients and contacts needs to be consistent and in line with the company's values.

Once you have established a set of SOPs that work for your particular situation, I suggest charging someone with looking at it once a year to keep it updated, as well as whenever you make a significant change in your business game plan.

As I shared with you at the start, multimillion-dollar magic requires a specific set of actions which you **do without fail** – THAT's how you will build to the numbers you dream of reaching. 100%.

Multimillion Dollar Magic: TAKEAWAYS

The "magic" that can build your business to multimillion dollar levels is based on identifying and committing to a specific combination of actions which you do *without fail* that will build and build to the numbers you dream of reaching.

Personal meaning means financial success.

- Use your Big Bold Vision to articulate what's meaningful to you in your business, vision, mission, values. Believe in it to sustain your motivation and energy to follow through on your plans.
- Reject any excuses that keep you from moving forward on your Big Bold Vision. You don't have to have all the answers before you can take specific actions that will take you to the next steps you need to take.

Lead with an unstoppable strategy.

Make a Business Growth Game Plan that forms the foundation of your strategy, decisions, and benchmarking with these guidelines in hand:

- Look at a holistic picture of your business.
- Build into your plan your priorities and the things that are most important to you.
- Plan your capacity for growth.
- Dare to make brilliant course corrections. Start with a solid plan, commit to action, assess and measure, then be willing to make adjustments as you go.

Tap into your resources and use them consistently, confidently, regularly.

Match your processes and systems with your new growth goals for the main function areas of your business.

- Include the expertise of your team and trusted professionals to help make the changes and upgrades.
- Match your SOPs to your new processes and systems.
- Tap into your people, and your relationships with them, as part of your growth plan.
- Build into your Business Growth Game Plan specific actions that you take every single day to nurture and develop your people resources.

BUSINESS GROWTH PLAN WORKSHEET

INSTRUCTIONS: To start your 5-year plan, explore these questions thoroughly – first with yourself, then adapt them to working with your leadership team.

1. What are we doing efficiently this year? (Celebrate that!)

_____

_____

_____

2. What are the hurdles that have stopped our business from achieving goals in the past?

_____

_____

_____

3. What are the top strategies we'll have in place [by year-end, next year, in 5 years...] that we'll look back on as successful?

_____

_____

_____

4. Are we building our business from a place of joy? (Yes, that's a zinger...)

_____

_____

_____

BUSINESS GROWTH GAME PLAN CHECKLIST

INSTRUCTIONS: Get a holistic picture of your business through these 9 steps. Keep accountability by noting the dates of initiation and completion.

STEP	TASK	START DATE	END DATE
☐ 1	**Translate your personal Big Bold Vision** into your company's North Star.		
☐ 2	**Outline the company vision** and general goals for the next five years. I find a 5-year plan most practical and actionable, considering rapid technological advances and global changes.		
☐ 3	**Revisit and pinpoint your market** and who your ideal customers are.		
☐ 4	**Update your UVP** (Unique Value Proposition) – what you offer like nobody else.		
☐ 5	**Update, clarify, and recommit** to your marketing and sales strategies.		

STEP	TASK	START DATE	END DATE
☐ 6	**Establish your objectives,** tasks, and measures of success.		
☐ 7	**Assess your operations,** processes, and tech that will support your plans.		
☐ 8	**Map out several financial scenarios** to fulfill your vision and objectives over time.		
☐ 9	**Outline and agree on next action steps** for your leadership team and companywide.		

CHAPTER SIX

FAST FUTURE GROWTH (FOR YOUR TEAMS)

*"You might be the GOAT (Greatest Of All Time)
of your company, yet you only win when you have
a great team behind you.»*

—Ivy Slater

When you go to a football game, your focus is on the players, right? If you go to a ballet, you see only the dancers on the stage. When we're in the middle of these exciting experiences, we only see the stars – we don't consider the many hundreds of people who make it all possible.

Think about it. You don't have football without the regulation ball, playing field, helmets and pads, coaches, referees, broadcasters, the waterboy (or girl) who keeps the players from collapsing on the field in 90% humidity.

You don't have a ballet performance without the hand-sewn pointe shoes, artistic directors and musicians, trainers, stagehands, costume sewers, dressers and makeup artists. You are dancing in the dark if you don't have the stage lighting – and nobody will see your excellence.

If you want the best of the best in performance, whatever the field or industry, *every person on your team is integral to success.*

An idea is founded by a person. A rapid-growth company is built by the team that grows the idea.

The differentiator between the average business and the best of the best is the quality of your team and how it is positioned.

We're going to explore three keys to building a winning team positioned for fast future growth:

1. **Ensure every team member knows they have value and are respected by the company**

2. **Attract, build and position your best-of-the-best team**

3. **Make it a company goal to train your leaders of tomorrow**

Three crucial steps to show your people they are a valued and respected part of your company's growth

This may seem obvious, but one of the most common things I find working with clients is that the right hand doesn't know what the left hand is doing – literally! This silo mentality can happen for a lot of reasons and not always intentionally. But it WILL hold a company back from rapid and sustained growth.

Visionary Action Step #1:
Develop your leadership team through the lens of THE BEST.

As a dancer, I always marveled at how the choreographer could bring everyone together to understand the vision and learn the dance movements and interpretations. Like the football coach's X's and O's game plan, it's a feat of leadership to get everyone on the team – top down – onto the same page.

Accomplishing this for your company's growth starts with your leadership team.

1) *Your goals and numbers drive everything – nail these down first.* Once you have built your company's vision and opportunity into the profitability picture, the next step is to assess *what, and who,* you need to make that happen.

Gather your leadership/exec team together to assess the company's growth needs based on the Business Growth Game Plan you have created. Consider engaging an expert to take you through this self-assessment process, and help you through those almost-inevitable tough conversations your team is going to have.

The outcome you want is to get answers to crucial questions like these:

- *Where are you getting resources and assistance? What are you delegating?*
- *Where are the gaps in resources in areas such as tech, funding, and attracting the right people?*
- *Is the leadership in your organization solid, or do you need to add expertise, shuffle responsibilities, or let someone go if there's not a fit?*

2) *Talk to your leadership team members about THEIR goals.* What I'm about to tell you strikes straight at the silo mentality problem that so many companies suffer from.

It's natural for leaders to think that because their leadership/exec team is on board with the company, it means **they're on board with everything** (or, if they're not there yet it's their job to get there). Not always so! This is a dangerous assumption that can backfire and block forward-growth motion.

I find that the best way to assess where your leadership/exec team stands is to actually connect with each person on the team privately to find out these things:

- What direction they're looking to go in support of their personal goals.
- Why getting there is important to them.

- What their thoughts are on the current vision and plans.

What you're doing here is ensuring you have a leadership/exec team that will **do what it takes to go to bat on behalf of the company and for themselves, because it's the same future**.

If your leadership team is already at that place, KUDOS! And have the conversations anyway because:

- It serves as an affirmation for each member that you're in this together.
- The company goals will shine even more clearly.
- Your team and individual relationships will deepen.

If it's not the case, you are doing your team an enormous favor by caring enough to explore their personal paths now, so they can be sure they're on the right track for their future as well as your company's future.

> **Ivy's Office Hours:** I was on a call with Morgan, CEO of a company that had just completed an M&A deal. They came to me with this concern:
>
> *Ivy, we're starting something really big here, combining our leadership and cultures and all the high expectations of the growth markets we're planning to tap. It's such a big chance, and I want to make sure I have the leadership team that's going to take us forward.*
>
> *As much as I like my exec team, I'm not sure they all are the right fit for this new chapter. They've all done great work, but NONE of them has what I'd call a boardroom presence or leadership skills. I feel like I need to make changes in the team or bring these folks up to speed to lead. What do I do?*
>
> Me: *Tell me more about what you're looking for to help them.*
>
> Morgan: *Well, Tina, our chief human resources officer (CHRO) suggested we engage you as a consultant for the exec team to bring them onboard*

as the leaders they need to be. She's thinking of a coaching call once a month – can you do that?

Me: *Yes, that's absolutely something I could do – if you're just checking a box to prove you brought in an expert to partner with your new team. But my showing up on a monthly call is not going to shift the culture of the exec team to become the leaders you're looking for. This is a matter of behavioral change, which is going to take time.*

They decided to move forward with me, and the first thing I did was start working with Tina so she could see how this process would go with the team members. I started by asking her to tell me a little about herself, and learned she'd been with the company for eight years, had a husband and three children.

Me: *So, it's safe to say that when your oldest goes off to college, this company will be in a very different place, right?*

Tina: *Yes, very ... I haven't even thought that far ahead.*

Me: *I'm sure! Well, how do you see your career at that point? What do you want it to look like?*

Tina: *In all the companies I've worked at, nobody's ever asked me that.*

We went on to explore what she personally expected to happen with this M&A (these conversations are of course confidential so she knew she could speak freely with me.) We discussed what she saw as her stake in the company's future now and what she was working toward – for her kids, retirement, and where she wanted to live.

What we were exploring was her personal vision and if it would be a match with the future this company was moving toward. And then we discussed the big questions: What does the new direction mean to her, and will it be worth it?

Tina understood in a new way what would inform her own decisions about her place in the company. She realized the value of these in-depth conversations to bring the exec team up to speed to meet the expectations of the merged company, as well as their own prospects.

I anticipated that some of them would want to stay and do what it would take to upgrade their leadership skills. Others would self-select to go in another direction, or Morgan and the new leadership would decide who wasn't going to be a fit for the new direction of the company.

A few months in, as of this writing I'm already seeing positive changes in the way many of them are ready to learn to be better leaders, because they're invested in being part of the company's future. A couple are planning to leave the company, and I'm confident they'll know it's a better move for their future.

3) *Revisit* your org culture to see if it still matches your leadership team's vision, and if it will support your people to be successful. You will be checking it against item #1, the goals and numbers that are driving this whole thing, and #2, the internal culture leadership has decided on.

> *"Many companies have a slogan. Very few companies bring that slogan to life, and that's why it's important to have the culture aligned with the values and then the behaviors aligned with that."*
> —**John Wallis,** *Chair at Rule No.1 sustainable consulting*[22]

These are the three main areas to look at:

- ***Clearly articulated core values*** that underpin everything the company is and does
- ***Standards of behavior***, not just on a legal basis in your policies but also vision-driven company expectations of how people treat each other as well as outfacing

- ***Clear communication avenues and systems*** so everyone can feel part of the growth project, and will have the information they need to be their best

It's especially important to embed this process by having your team recommit to the new org culture and policies you've agreed upon. Why? Because when your leadership practices stem from common values, standards and purpose, they send a clear message to everyone – and I mean everyone (including the water boy/girl!). *THIS is what the best of the best looks like.*

Take an active role in attracting, hiring and positioning your best-of-the-best team

With your leadership team in place, now fill in those gaps that will take you where you want your company to go by bringing in the people you need, and supporting them every step of the way to personal and company success.

"Top of the flywheel for us is to surround ourselves with the right people with the right talent. Our core value is to work with and empower them to achieve their personal, professional, and financial goals. When we do this right, we're going to win no matter what challenges come our way." ~Ron Alvesteffer, President and CEO of Service Express.[23]

Visionary Action Step #2:
Find and retain the right, best people.

Do the numbers, keep it simple, and get creative. Match your needs with the numbers by answering these questions:

- *Do we need help? If so, what does that look like:*
  - » *A virtual assistant (VA) or administrative team?*
  - » *Bringing in a consultant, coach, or other biz dev specialist?*

- » *Expanding our sales or marketing team?*
- » *More research and development (R&D) specialists or other experts, either outsourced or salaried?*

- *Are there people who are not adding value to the organization? Could this money be better invested for greater value elsewhere? If we go the route of separation, what will it cost and what will be left to allocate for new talent?*
- *Here's one for YOU (and perhaps ask your leadership/exec team members about their individual needs): Do I need support in my personal life so I can be my very best?*

How do you look at your numbers to hire somebody?

The answer to this question could fill the pages of another book! What I want to share with you here is that it doesn't have to be complicated – I'm all about simplifying things for my clients because they're always busy. When you ask the questions above and compare different financial scenarios, you can get creative about solving your resource needs in the best possible ways.

Ivy's Office Hours: Jordan was managing partner of a boutique law firm he founded in Atlanta. His high-level work and specialty area had clients banging down his doors on a regular basis. He and his partners were working seven days a week, and they'd been running in this hamster wheel for months.

We started by looking at his current team and their strengths. Sometimes you need to hire, and sometimes you need to delegate within your teams to help your people focus on what they are best at.

Jordan: *The partners have never had that conversation, per se – we all kind of understand "who does what" in terms of casework. Angela, for example, is fantastic at contracts but, you know, I've never asked her if she likes to do them!*

So, we agreed that he would discuss with his partners how the work could be distributed more effectively *and happily* for them; and where there might be gaps in some strengths they want to fill to better serve their client base and grow the firm.

Then we tackled another money-wasting aspect ...

Me: *Jordan, I want you to do a little exercise. For the next two weeks I'd like you to keep a list of what you do every day and track all of your time.*

Jordan (BIG eye roll): *You know us attorneys – we are always tracking our time! What more do you want me to do?*

Me: *I want you to capture the practical and specific details as well as the actual billed work. It's just for two weeks. Make it as detailed as possible; I can help you set up a method to make it easiest for you.*

After the two weeks, color code all the things on the list according to these three categories: the things you don't want to do anymore; the things you might like to do but are incredibly time consuming; and the things you love to do most.

He agreed, and two weeks later we met to go over his list. Here's part of our conversation:

Jordan: *So, I spend a lot of time relationship building, like networking and speaking to groups. I'd really love to delegate that but I know I can't – so much for that ...*

Me: *Well, not necessarily! You can't always delegate your in-person relationship building, but you can delegate keeping track of your activities such as scheduling, reminder calls or texts, writing simple standard follow-up touchpoints, paying your dues and memberships, etc. It would also be great to bring in someone to support some of your relationship building on social media.*

Jordan: *I could do that. Maybe one of my two part-time assistants could help. Georgette is really good at client contacts. But both say they're so busy.*

Me: *Great idea! Do you know if either of them would welcome adding some hours to their week?*

Jordan: *Hm ... I never thought to ask them. I know Georgette's working to put her daughter through college. Maybe she'd like more hours.*

We found a couple of other responsibilities that he didn't mind doing but could be delegated to one of the assistants. Jordan also suggested consulting his partners to see if they had enough work to delegate to Georgette if she wanted a full-time position.

These three small tweaks to Jordan's organizational structure brought big rewards – financially and in terms of peace of mind. The partners began using each other's talents more and even inspired a case-sharing arrangement with a colleague which increased referrals to their specialty work. They saved money by focusing on what they do and love best, and were more relaxed at work. Georgette was grateful to come on full-time with a raise, which saved money on the search and training they would have had to do to make a new hire.

Remember that when you hire, it's more than the numbers. You can measure skills, experience, education, and compensation by the numbers – but you can't measure character and personality.

Ensure success by including in your candidate interviews questions and conversations that will help you get to know their values, character, what's most important to them, personal and professional goals, etc. (of course, after making sure you're compliant with Equal Employment Opportunity Commission and other state and federal labor laws). It will be time well spent, I promise you, and the first step to building a relationship that may result in tomorrow's leader.

"I involve my team in all of my hiring decisions. I do
the initial interview, then I hand it over to my team to take
the person to lunch. There's a better chance they'll all play in
the sandbox well together."
—**Susan Graham,** *President of Susan Graham Consulting LLC*[24]

Pursuing the best of the best is your best guarantee of sustainable growth!

Visionary Action Step # 3:
Give your people the tools they need
to thrive in their job.

As we see from the example of Morgan's exec team, the people you hire, whether it's from the outside or promoting from within, may not have all the skills and tools they need to thrive in their position.

What if they have no experience in the aspects of leadership that truly define success, such as the ability to have difficult conversations, motivate a team, build their people up, perform their job with confidence?

Don't expect that they'll figure it out on their own (even if you have them read this book!). They are already dealing with the new position, increased responsibility, higher compensation and potentially more stress. They may have worked wonderfully as a solo employee, but never had to manage people under them while still navigating their own workload.

They're now in a whole different ball game, and need the support of the organization.

1) The Visionary Leader takes the responsibility to develop their people, not just hire them or throw them the bone of a promotion then walk away. Build into their transition process the opportunities for them to develop the skills they need to thrive in their new role. Here are some suggestions to get you started:

> Assign another leader to mentor them for the first few months in their new role, doing some proactive training and/or making themselves available for questions and guidance.

> Invite them to attend high-level meetings to see how the top tier of the organization operates; have them shadow more experienced leaders at their meetings.

Make it a group training effort: Arrange new managers to get together to read a business book or listen to a podcast together, then discuss what they've learned and how they will implement better practices into their day.

2) *Bring in an outside coach to do the training.* Often clients tell me that everyone is too busy with their own responsibilities to train others. I understand that challenge. Engaging an independent expert can be a great help in these ways:

Special expertise and tools to help your new leader determine the type of leader they desire to be, then work with them on developing the skill sets and nuances to own their own leadership style.

Serving as an objective third party may help your new leader feel more at ease, safe and free to make mistakes without reprisal.

Saving money and preserving productivity by not diverting your people with this added responsibility!

3) *Build leadership training into your operations and org culture.* Don't treat leadership training as an ad hoc, one-and-done kind of thing. Spend time and resources to develop a system to use with each new hire, as well as any employees who show an interest and potential for moving into leadership roles.

Once the training system is in place, it can be used over and over on an individual or group level. You could create an internal resource group with a focus on developing leaders.

"We train our people how to take ownership of any type of client situation. Every Friday we pick a topic like accountability or client service. This week's topic is listening. We provide a platform and resources for our people to really own their professional life and to own their responsibilities within the firm."
—**Nancy Rizzuto,** *Founding Partner and Principal, CAP STRAT*[25]

What incredible ways to value and nurture your greatest asset – your people!

How to find, nurture and train tomorrow's leaders

Ready for a reality check? ***Everyone's replaceable – even you!*** Let me explain ...

My company, Slater Graphics, was in the throes of an extremely busy season when I got a call that my dad was in the hospital. Although he was getting up in age he had been healthy, and we had just left him the previous Saturday after spending several wonderful days together. Hours later he had collapsed and was rushed to the hospital.

I knew it was possible that Monday my company would be opening its doors without me. I called my business partner on the way to the hospital to tell him I had no idea what I'd be walking into or how long I would be needed. Because of the cross-functional system we had set up long before, by the end of the conversation we had the next month covered.

My dad passed quietly on Sunday morning. I was incredibly grateful that I could be where I was needed – with my family – and the work would be taken care of.

In my situation, my partner and I had an entirely separate set of clients in quite different industries. We created a policy where all our clients knew each of us and we knew the status of every job in our business. Therefore, I knew my partner could step into my shoes with almost no information from me, giving me the opportunity to focus on my family without added stress. I could do the same for him, and our staff knew they could depend on this policy to support them as well.

Life happens in moments, some wonderful and some unfortunate. As a Visionary Leader you have to make preparations in your company for those unexpected times when one of your people is called away, or to replace a top leader/partner so that the company doesn't collapse. You also need to plan for your employees' capability to take scheduled time off for vacations, Parental leave, sabbaticals, etc.

It's worth mentioning because too many times I see clients who run growing professional services companies, absorbed in the weeds of work, and they have not made proper preparations to replace an employee, leader or partner if something unexpected happens. They suddenly get blindsided, chaos ensues, and setbacks and unhappy customers happen.

There's a saying that you should be planning for your replacement the day you start a new job, and I believe it's true!

Why does planning to replace your people ensure fast future growth for your teams? Because creating a system of cross-functional training not only helps keep the systems running smoothly, it also helps:

- Your people feel valued and taken care of.
- Leadership/management to identify potential talent and leadership skills in their people.
- Bring everyone together with a greater sense of context, unity and common vision.

Visionary Action Step # 4:
Find and nurture your leaders of tomorrow.

1) When you establish leadership training as part of your operations and org culture as suggested earlier, you are already on your way to preparing all of your people with the skills and knowledge that will allow them to step into a leadership role when it's needed.

Along with this training, find opportunities to cross-train in certain vital tasks and across functions, especially on management and team lead levels.

2) *With your leadership, exec or management team, discern:*

- *Who are my leaders of tomorrow?*
- *What skills do we need to help them develop or hone?*
- *How can we organize this cross-training in a systematic way?*

3) *Choose those people with leadership potential* to personally nurture and train, which will serve your vision and growth in these ways and more:

- Keeping your company running smoothly when the unexpected happens.
- Being ready to promote from within with more assurance that they will be ready for their next-level leadership role.
- Developing them with the capacity to meet their own professional vision and goals, which helps them thrive and strive to be their best.

4) *Personal note to you new leaders:* When you find yourself in a leadership position that's new to you, it can feel daunting! Consider this:

- Believe you are there for a reason. Someone saw your potential and gave you that responsibility.
- Know you are never alone. Even though you are the one leading, you can still do as much listening and learning as you did in any other role. A great leader becomes great because of this very habit.
- Be vulnerable enough to listen to your team(s) and learn from them. Not only will you accelerate your learning curve, they will appreciate you for tapping into their expertise!

Fast Future Growth (for your teams): TAKEAWAYS

The differentiator between the average business and the best of the best is the quality of your team and how it's positioned.

Three keys to a winning team positioned for rapid growth:

#1: *Every team member knows they have value and respect for their part in the company's growth.*

- Develop your team through the lens of THE BEST, starting at the top.
- Embed in your org culture the expectations, behaviors, and values that will bring out excellence in everyone

#2: *Leadership takes a proactive role in team building and nurturing*

- Find and retain the right, best people.
- Give your people the tools they need to thrive in their job.

#3: *Training tomorrow's leaders is a company goal.*

- To build strong leadership in your organization, you have to antici-pate that every person is replaceable. Build in plans and cross-func-tional capabilities to keep things running smoothly, no matter what.
- Find and nurture your leaders of tomorrow. Identify who your po-tential leaders are, what skills they need to develop or hone; and how best to train them in these areas, in a systemic way.

LEADERSHIP TEAM INDIVIDUAL GOALS WORKSHEET

INSTRUCTIONS: This is your personal worksheet to help you assess your professional and personal goals. Answer each question honestly and thoroughly.

1. What do I want my personal life to look like in 5 years? In 10 years? Prompts: location, family, travel, 2nd home, personal interests, etc.

_____

_____

_____

2. What do I want my professional life to look like in 5 years? In 10 years? Prompts: in this firm, position, role and responsibilities, change in career, further education, retirement, etc.

_____

_____

_____

3. What is most important to me in my professional life? Prompts: leadership (what level), expertise, meaningful livelihood, money, lifestyle, legacy, etc.

_____

_____

_____

4. In what ways is this current situation meeting my goals?

_____

_____

_____

5. What gaps are there between what I want professionally and what this firm is offering me?

_____

_____

_____

6. Do I believe in the company's core values and plans for the future? Why, why not, or which aspects?

_____

_____

_____

CHAPTER SEVEN

FUTURE FORWARD MARKETING

"The best companies and the best leaders are always looking forward. And they're always staying ahead of the curve in terms of where things are going three, four or five years down the road."

—**Laura Held,** Partner at Shamrock Capital

For my clients who want to grow or shift their market direction, the biggest obstacle they face is their own limited perspective on marketing. In these cases, I welcome the chance to open their minds!

At some point, most leaders I know (myself included) find themselves stuck in the same marketing strategies, resourcing the same activities, and targeting the same markets – and discovering they're not getting the results they desire anymore.

To run with the best of the best, the Visionary Leader is constantly vigilant about the market they're serving and how they are reaching that market, especially since the marketplace can change so quickly and the competition in today's world does too.

"Whenever there's a new widget out on the market – like protecting your privacy on your phone or getting insurance on your drones that do photography – we jump in and get known for that! People will come to us and say, 'Hey, I have this thing." How do I deal with it?' So, we learn about it, and try

to do the right thing by our clients by offering it." ~Susan L. Combs, CEO at Combs & Company, LLC, and Founder of Pancakes for Roger Inc.[26]

We're going to explore three key considerations to spark new marketing ideas that will boost your competitive edge:

1. **Niche customer targeting**

2. **"Transformational Ties" that last – and pay**

3. **Networking as a marketing strategy**

Niche customer targeting opens next-level opportunities – if you choose to see them!

When you tap into your Inner Visionary, you can spot market possibilities you never thought of before which could become lucrative for the company and game-changing for you.

> **When I started selling for the printing business,** I needed to find new ways to create sales that outperformed my peers. Those peers were men; printing was a male-dominated industry at the time. It was a struggle even to get a call back once people heard my feminine voice on the phone. I asked myself: *Where are the holes in the marketplace?*
>
> Well, it became as plain as the high heels on my feet: *Women!*
>
> I first saw that the holes in the printing industry marketplace were women decision makers who weren't being leveraged. Then I realized that many women-owned and women-targeted companies were also being ignored. This opened many doors for me, which I happily stepped through!

Niche-customer targeting opened up everything for me, and led me to taking over the company within three years, attaining seven figures, and realizing year-over-year profits.

Visionary Action Step #1:
Match your passions and strengths to
the needs of the marketplace.

For any business, regardless of size or industry, you need to figure out what it is that you do extremely well – better than other people. Then focus on that.

It feels like a pretty simple concept, doesn't it? But like so many aspects of our inner game, we're often reluctant to explore new options because:

- The current (outdated) business culture rarely supports us doing the things we love to do and are really good at. Instead, we're often expected to fit our round "pegs" in square "holes" in order to be successful.

   It doesn't – shouldn't – have to be that way.

- This culture also supports doing more, making more, reaching more, leveraging more, which can cause us to lose our sense of discernment and focus. We believe that if we choose a niche, we'll miss all the opportunities outside of that niche – we'll lose out if we choose one alternative over another.

   So, we go general and spread ourselves thin, which doesn't work because *the more ground we try to cover, the more diffuse our impact becomes.* And the market becomes confused as to who we are and what we're about..

Niche customer targeting does not have to be an either-or situation. ***You'll make the most lucrative sales when you work from your own "best of the best" qualities, talents, and vision.***

Let's take another look at Jordan's law firm from Chapter Six. They had a steady feed of cases – great! However, our numbers showed that working with clients outside the firm's specialty was holding them back instead of moving them forward. They were reluctant to say *no* to any opportunity, and didn't realize that it was costing them more on admin, outsourcing paralegals, and on the partners' time than was profitable – to the tune of six figures a year plus high blood-pressure levels!

I helped them focus on growing what they *wanted to grow and to invest in that,* and let go of the cases that were costing them money while diluting their specialty brand. They began to look more openly at their market, and created cross-referral partnerships where they fed each other the niche clients each firm had targeted. So, they were not missing opportunities, they actually increased sales and profitability by niche-targeting.

Here are the process steps to ensure you're making the right choices:

1) *Find out what you are most passionate about in your business. Ask:*

- *When was a customer/client really satisfied with our service, and it made us so happy?*
- *What specific thing would I do even if I never got paid for it because I'm so passionate about it?*
- *What things do I do that I believe bring value as well as fulfill my purpose?*

When you lock into your passion and purpose, you 100X your chances of making great sales, because your influence and energy become irresistible. There is nothing like getting up in the morning with a smile on your face and a brisk step in your day because you're passionate about what you are doing, and you know you're great at it. (Talk about 17Xing confidence!)

2) *Take the pulse of the marketplace.* The marketplace is always shifting; set down some data points on what shifts and trends you/your team believe to be notable. Explore with your team:

- *Where are holes in the marketplace we can fill?*
- *What/who is underserved?*
- *How do we come in and solve those problems with the solutions that will continue to help them move forward?*
- *What are some ways we can go after that niche?*

"The only permanent thing is change. Keep your head up, embrace the change, make the most of it, and see how it can make you a better person, your team better and your company better."
—**Nicola "Nikki" Fraser,** *Managing Partner and Cofounder of NextKey Services*[27]

3) *Test your choices against the marketplace.* Be visionary, but also realistic – do not follow your own data points only.

What better way to find out what the needs are than by asking! Do a simple market research survey or questionnaire, or actually call and talk personally to a dozen or so clients, potential clients, and colleagues in complementary or vertical businesses, to find out what they're looking for. Ask questions such as:

- *What are the problems that you perceive have arisen in this marketplace?*
- *What do you need most in the area of [fill in the blanks]?*
- *What are the greatest gaps that prevent your business from thriving that you wish could be filled?*

4) *Make a short list of highest-potential niches*. Find the Venn-diagram commonalities between what you/your company do particularly well and which niches in the marketplace are not being served.

5) *Which, if any, of these niches are viable? DO THE NUMBERS* – not only in terms of quick gain but also of longer-term investment. Consider some questions and scenarios:

- *Can we sell this ourselves without added staff or admin?*
- *Do we need human or financial resources to make this work? What are the costs?*
- *Are there current targets that are doing worse than the new one we're testing in terms of cost and potential return? If so, what would it look like to phase out that current target and phase in our new one?*
- *What's the timeline and financial runway to make this shift?*

With each niche idea, you'll either learn that you're off the mark this time, or that it has potential with additions or reallocation of resources.

Make your decision:

Heck yeah, why didn't we think of this before?

Yes, but not yet.

Yes, and let's do x, y, and z to build it into our two-year plan.

Any one of these decisions are good – just make sure to follow through on whatever the decision turns out to be so you don't miss out on the opportunity.

How Transformational Ties make connections that last – and pay!

As I stated earlier, true success in business is no longer measured just by how well you transact deals; it is how well you build relationships – what I like to call **Transformational Ties** – that inspire, motivate, and help others be their best selves, and which reap returns on many levels.

At Slater Graphics, one of the first major niche clients I landed was Chantelle, an intimates company, who hired us to produce and deliver B2B catalogs countrywide for all the big department stores like Bloomingdale's, Saks Fifth Avenue and Neiman Marcus.

Each job had custom specs and was highly complex from design to printing to drop shipping.

My contact, Laurie, was a person with exacting taste, laser attention to details, and high expectations. Things were going fine for several years until the "job from hell" happened, where something seemed to go wrong every step of the way.

Laurie was not happy with the final product. At the end of that job, when she and I sat down to discuss all that had happened, Laurie concluded, "I like you a lot as a person, Ivy, but I can't use you any more as a vendor."

It was devastating for me and a significant loss of more than $100,000 in today's dollars. Yet I knew it wasn't personal. And I appreciated how much I'd learned from the experience, which I was able to put back into the company later as CEO. I didn't burn my bridges with her (which is my Number One rule in doing business). Besides, I liked her personally too.

Over the next several years I kept up with what Laurie was doing. When I learned that she had left Chantelle for a career step forward, I reached out to congratulate her, and we decided to meet for coffee. Laurie greeted me with a warm hug and peck on the cheek, and we sat down to a friendly conversation.

I shared with her my new venture, Slater Success, and what my future plans were for the company. She was excited for me and asked a lot of questions. Then she implored me to join her the next day for a breakfast event at a nonprofit she was involved with, Dress for Success.

Honestly, money was a bit tight then as I'd just started my company, and it was a $100-dollar breakfast (*and* I'm not a breakfast-food fan!). But she was so enthusiastic I couldn't resist.

How surprised was I to arrive in a ballroom packed with more than 500 women! There was nothing to do but be bold and go up and introduce myself, and I was struck by how impressive this group of professional women was. Eventually Laurie spotted me in the crowd and came over to say hello. Then she grabbed me by the hand and said, "I need to introduce you to someone. She's going to be your client."

Well, she turned out to be correct. I started working with the young woman, who had just stepped into the position of Director of Development for a long-established education nonprofit. The staff and board were really putting her through the paces.

Through our work together, Suzanne shifted from being overrun by her people to exceeding all of that year's fundraising goals by the end of her first anniversary with the organization.

Laurie and I worked together often over the years: I created a group coaching structure for her and her corporate colleagues; advised her and helped with negotiations when she was approached by a prestigious global company; and ran workshops and did individual coaching for the new firm she ended up joining.

It's been such an honor to work with Laurie and know her as a friend. This incredible woman was eventually appointed president of one of the company's affiliate brands for North and South America – the first woman to accomplish this feat.

One relationship led to over seven figures' worth of business for her, and set my new company on the path to our own milestone earning levels!

Why do Transformational Ties work?

We think we do business with companies. We actually do business with people.

If you think about a great customer experience you have had, it was likely because of the people who served you. Conversely, if you had a terrible customer experience it was likely due to the people you dealt with much more than the product or brand itself.

Today business is done through "know, like, and trust," and this is achieved **through intentional, strategic relationship building.** It's an essential marketing tool that blends service, marketing and sales. And it's … well … transformational!

How to make networking a key part of your marketing strategy

Networking is the process of interacting and engaging with people for mutual benefit, usually in an informal social setting (versus scheduled sales appointments or cold calling). It's an excellent way to develop meaningful Transformational Ties, especially in the professional services world. Yet it's often overlooked as a valuable marketing/sales tool, so we don't give it the attention, intention, planning, and follow-up that will reap big rewards over time.

> *"My network is my net worth."*
> —**Joi Gordon,** *cofounder of Rapport Inc.*
> *and Gordon Hewes Consulting*[28]

Networking opportunities can be found almost anywhere – informally at the coffee shop, your kid's baseball game, dinner parties, clubs, etc.; more formally through networking groups, business associations, and volunteer/ nonprofit groups.

With formal associations, choose carefully to make sure your ideal potential clients will be there, otherwise it can become a burdensome (and expensive) rabbit hole with nothing to show for the effort (believe me, I've been there…).

Once you do commit, go all-in with them, allowing time for the ties to form and develop. This is an example of how it can work:

In my networking group on a recent Wednesday night (I've been with them for several years), when someone asked: *Hey, Ivy, do you have an ask?* It was easy: *Yes, I'm looking for three great introductions. My goal is to land two clients of x caliber by x time period.*

The group asked me a few more questions and said, *Sure, you got it!* I knew they would look out for me in the same way I would for them (reciprocity is an important factor in this equation). They were motivated because they knew me, liked me, and trusted me. And I got my introductions.

How to start and nurture those Transformational Ties that last and pay?

Visionary Action Step #2:
Make your connections about them, not about you.

When you meet people, the first step is to find those things they can relate to and that resonate with you as well. This helps them feel heard, valued, and safe (important ingredients of the trust piece).

The secret, as Dale Carnegie famously advised, is to **be more interest-ED than interest-ING.**[29] (By the way, when I started in sales in my mid 20's, my father told me to read Dale Carnegie – thanks, Dad, that was great advice!). To me this means approaching people with sincere interest in who they are, rather than starting out of the gate with assumptions you've made about them or, worse, focusing on "selling" yourself.

How? **See them as individuals, not your next sales number.** Get curious and ask questions. Find out what you have in common. Then you'll know what to share about yourself, and what else to ask them.

See if you feel any excitement about the potential ties you may have with this person, anywhere from becoming a client, to employee to partner to referral source to best friend. Then you can decide if you want to part ways or take the encounter to the next level.

Visionary Action Step #3:
Plan your networking experience and desired outcomes ahead of time.

1) *Be prepared.* Go to any networking/association/speaking opportunity equipped with a few thoughtful opening questions, something more creative than the usual, *So, what do you do?* It doesn't have to be about business – personal is more engaging and begins to build "know, like, trust."

Take a cue from the season of the year, location of the venue, or something current that's going on (not political or controversial, of course). Example: A sports tournament is about to happen near the hotel whose meeting room you're in. Start the conversation with something like: *Have you seen how many people are here for the tournament? Do you follow this sport? Have you seen famous players since you came to town?*

2) *Be present.* Whether you identify as an introvert or extrovert, it can feel a little daunting and uncomfortable to enter the room of a networking event or conference.

- Before an event, acknowledge to yourself if it's feeling uncomfortable or not your favorite thing to go into a room and approach strangers. Then, shift that thinking by *also* acknowledging the excitement of meeting someone who could become the best customer you've ever had!
- Show up 100% *you*. Don't worry about being the perfect professional. We want to do business with real people, not automatons. Someone who comes across as "perfect" with all the answers can actually feel off-putting or intimidating.

3) *Be REAL...yet strategic.* Are you thinking, *How do I do all this? Seems like a lot of effort and follow-up and time!* I've got your back...

When I first thought about starting Slater Success, I followed up just about every single lead I was exposed to. I was cordial enough when I met them, but I didn't know how to get to know them well enough to decide whether

I wanted to take the next step. Nor did I know how to engage them so they could get to know me too.

Until I developed the approach I'm about to describe, I wasted more time than I can count going to coffees that went nowhere fast!

Here are some practical strategies to help you manage it all:

- Don't walk "cold" into any networking opportunity – prepare ahead by determining what you want to get out of the experience: *Who will be there – are they likely my people? Is it worth my time?*

- Get clear on the outcome you desire. Maybe for this one it's not clients per se, but referral sources, potential vendors or professionals from a certain industry, or volunteers for your side passion of community service.

- Based on your intended outcome, prepare your focused questions and follow-ups so you can ask, listen carefully, follow up, and get a good idea if you want to continue this conversation or connection. If the person isn't feeling right to you, make a polite exit!

- My personal rule of thumb: *Do they make me smile?* I have to enjoy the conversation – because I have to enjoy working with them down the road.

4) Do the numbers (you guessed it)! We talked about this a bit with the Pure Profit Equation. Networking as a marketing strategy can have fuzzy boundaries: Are you selling? Are you socializing? Is it just a "cost of doing business" you have to expect and accept? Yes, yes – and no!

In the Pure Profit Equation, you must have a marketing line item for networking to quantify the time, expense and effort that you or your team are devoting to this important marketing tool.

Have you ever kept track of the costs involved? And if you are tracking, have you deducted those business expenses? To help you know what to track, ask these questions:

- How much am I spending on dues, memberships and association fees?

- How many lunches, coffees, etc., have I paid for this year; and how much money have I spent?
- How much TIME am I spending doing the networking – planning, preparing, attending and following up? Estimate what that might be costing you.
- The crucial question: Has it been worth it?

I've gotten very discerning about the potential revenue I could receive from networking compared to my investment. Once I had a handle on my network marketing strategy, I made sure I spent my time and money wisely. In one instance, a $500 outlay over two years brought in a $100,000 client – good investment? I'd say yes!

Future Forward Marketing: TAKEAWAYS

Niche customer targeting opens next-level opportunities – if you choose to see them.

- Tap into your Inner Visionary to spot market possibilities you never thought of before.
- Match your passions and strengths to your customer's greatest needs.
- Do the numbers and assess the costs, including the human ones, to find out what will fly.

Transformational Ties make connections that last – and pay.

- Seven-figure selling is done through intentional, strategic relationship building.
- Make your connections with people about them, not about you. Prepare creative questions that will lay the groundwork for a "know, like, trust" relationship.

- Be prepared for your conversations (it's a great confidence builder); be vulnerable to reach people on a personal level; be REAL as your authentic self.

Make networking an official part of your marketing strategy.

- Give networking the attention and planning it deserves to reward you with lucrative Transformational Ties. Choose your networking groups and associations carefully, then go all-in. Make every connection count!
- Be strategic about developing an efficient as well as an effective approach. Ensure that you and your team are clear on: the intention of your networking experience; desired outcome; and the types of connections you want to make and develop.
- Do the numbers! Make networking and other marketing strategies a line item in your budget to ensure you're not wasting money on ineffectual efforts. Capture those numbers and business deductions.

NETWORKING STRATEGY CHECKLIST

INSTRUCTIONS: To schedule your networking activities for the next 90 days (also useful for meeting planning), break them down according to these considerations. Use the chart below for each event you attend:

Event Name:

_____

1. What do I want to get out of this event?

_____

_____

_____

2. Who will be there, how many?

_____

_____

_____

3. List the time and costs:

_____

_____

_____

4. Prep some questions to ask to support intended outcomes:

_____

_____

_____

5. Results:

_____

_____

_____

Keep this checklist to help track your activities, time and dollar cost, and any successful results.

CHAPTER EIGHT
SEVEN FIGURE SELLING

"As a leader, people are looking to you to figure things out. So be curious, always be learning, always be growing. Invest in the people who can help you figure it out. You'll be amazed at what you can achieve over time!"

—**Ron Alvesteffer,** President and CEO of Service Express

By definition, selling is the transaction where a good or service is being exchanged for money.

Sounds simple, right? You want a coffee, you choose the coffee shop that carries the coffee drinks you like best, the barista makes it, you pay them, and you're good to go.

That's not what this chapter is about, because I know that you know how to make a sale. I want to talk about jumping to those next levels that guarantee rapid growth to seven figures and beyond.

How do you reach those levels? Not through stress-producing, in-your-face selling and coercion but by being the ***visionary influencer who finds the right people and leads them to realize for themselves that YOU are the one they have been looking for!***

The first thing to acknowledge and embrace is this: As the price point gets higher, customer expectations get higher too because they want more value for the dollar they are investing. So, selling has to meet that level of expectation with a higher level of planning, engagement and time.

What does this mean to your sales? ***As you raise your growth goals you also have to uplevel your sales game*** – yours, your sales team's, and companywide.

There are three keys to seven-figure selling that separate the average from the best of the best:

1. **Play the long game (Transformational Ties Part 2)**

2. **Make your people rainmakers**

3. **Close your sales with the "Solution Conversation"**

This is not about training your sales team; we're going to focus on you the Visionary Leader as the foundational force who leads the way to fit these concepts into your company size, needs, and team structures. Then you can take it from there.

Playing the long game: Slow down for rapid growth

Take your time with rapid growth – counterintuitive, right? But it works as a way of growing your business. I've experienced this in my own businesses, and I help my clients reach seven figures and beyond.

The long game is to grow many Transformational Ties over time with intention, consistency and patience.

The long game will build a flow of business that has your company moving steadily forward. Over time these relationships you and your people forge will lead to a beautiful tipping point of loyal repeat business and regular high-quality referrals, which will increase your sales exponentially – and consistently.

As a bonus, you develop a reputation that positions you as the go-to expert in your space and as a thought leader, expanding your influence on legacy-making levels.

Caveat: I'm not suggesting that this approach is a substitute for your other marketing and sales strategies. Each business is different in terms of the best ways to reach and convert their target market. So, keep up whatever you're doing that is working for you!

However, I'm a strong believer that even if your business development comes from online marketing, **combining it with the offline engagement wins the seven-figure game.** Think about:

- What you are doing to support and nurture your customers on an ongoing basis.
- What you could be doing better in terms of developing Transformational Ties.
- If your online leads are down, seriously assess how you can improve your offline networking, follow-up and follow-through.

Visionary Action Step #1:
Follow up and follow through with your
Transformational Ties.

I often hear comments like these from my clients:

"I feel awkward calling people only when I need something."

"I feel hesitant to reach out with an urgent need or a new offer when I haven't contacted this person for months."

"If I contact them, aren't they always just going to think I want to sell them something?"

I understand their concern – it's what *transactional* relationships look like. Instead of thinking about a connection only in a moment of need or when it comes time to launch a sales campaign, **build a connection with them in a consistent, strategic and systematic way from the start.**

If this feels daunting to even consider, let me inspire you with this great example of the easiest, most satisfying sale ever – exactly what I want you to experience on a regular basis!

> **Ivy's Office Hours:** I was at a function some years ago where I met Tanya. I did my usual, asking her questions out of curiosity. We found some things in common during that short conversation and parted cordially.
>
> About six months later I spotted her at another event and went over to say hello. We got to talking and realized that we lived about ten blocks away from each other in Manhattan! We parted, saying we'd have to meet for coffee one morning before work.
>
> I followed up with her, and we met a couple of weeks later at a breakfast place between our two apartments. It wasn't long before we found that we both love the theater and talked about our favorite plays, someone she knows who has ticket packages (*That sounds interesting…Does it? Then let me introduce you to my contact*) and so on.
>
> Then Tanya said: *Let's talk business for a second.*
>
> Me: *Great.* I asked her a few questions about her firm, then I saw her literally take her Amex card out and slide it across the table toward me.
>
> I thought, oh, she's picking up the coffees…how nice. But before I could say anything (fortunately), she said: *You know, Ivy, I've been following you since we first met – scrolling your website, listening to your podcasts, reading your social media posts, and all of that. But I really wanted to get to know you better before I said yes.*
>
> *And now that I have, I want to work with you. Tell me what that would look like.*

Well...first, I checked to make sure my jaw wasn't still dropped down to my knees! Then I responded: *Okay, let's get into some questions...What is driving you right now?*

Tanya shared a few personal goals and activities she was involved in, adding: *I'm really ready to expand my firm in the next few years. And one thing I know is this – I've been doing everything I've been doing yet we're getting the same results. So, something has to change. I want to start blowing things up a little bit! I want to look at things with fresh eyes.*

Can you help me do that? And what would that look like?

(Music to my ears...) We continued to discuss her vision, goals, perceived problems, etc. Then we outlined a scope of work for the next 6 to 12 months.

Tanya: *This is great. Here's my credit card. Send me over a contract.*

Years later we're still working together, as she continues to take steps to make her business profitable, visionary, and reach her professional and personal goals.

See what happened there? It's the ideal result from playing the long game, meaning you don't have to "sell;" rather, you develop the relationship, pair it with value-driven marketing strategies, have your "Solution Conversation" (which we'll get to in a moment) and your service sells itself.

1) *Identify your clients and connections.* This is an important assignment to get you started on expanding your relationships. You'll want to treat this like any good SOP, supported by systems that will keep you organized and on task.

- **Make a list of:**
  - » Everyone you've ever had as a client, including in a former business or even back in school days.

> » Everyone you've known since you've been in business, whether or not you think they're a likely client.

Try for at least thirty names – really nudge your memory and pick your brain.

- **Pick the top 10%** of people from the list who could be:
  - » Potential new clients or business connections.
  - » Likely to know people who would be lucrative introductions for you.
  - » Referral sources to develop further.

- **Identify a select number of people out of that list** – a number you can hold yourself accountable to contact in a strategic, consistent way.
- **Connect to these people daily,** not each person daily but scheduled on a regular basis. Make it easy on yourself – use the media you like best, and set your systems up to support those choices.

Some creative prompts:

- *Send a quick note, referencing a mutually shared hobby or something you have in common. How's the softball league going? Wondering how your garden is looking these days…*
- *Send a video or link to a new series or documentary you think they will like, or info on something you know they're interested in. Thought you might be interested… Did you hear about [restaurant or museum] opening in your city?*
- *Once you both decide to keep the communication going, schedule an online or in-person get-together. I'm going to be speaking in Chicago next week - would you like to meet for coffee?*

- **Rinse and repeat, working through your list**, tagging on your CRM according to the nature of their relationship to you (referral source, client, vendor, etc.). It won't be long before it becomes a part of your daily routine, with enjoyable connections once you get the system down.

I can bet that you'll find there are more potential resources in your sphere than you ever thought possible. And I can guarantee that consistent and personal touchpoints with these people will reap valuable rewards!

2) Relationships require you to share YOU – sincere, genuine, personable, vulnerable, unique, brilliant. You know...your X Factor. I do *not* recommend relying only on AI and algorithms to represent the *real you*! I'm sure you know what I mean if you've ever received a "hi friend" online or text message from someone you've never heard of, or recognized swipe copy in a contact's email that doesn't sound a bit like them.

I cannot emphasize enough the personal aspect of sales – again, people deal with people, not companies. Along with the marketing data, strategies and systems, your personal values and intuition come into play, in terms of who you trust, who you resonate with, and who makes you feel cautious or even unmotivated to ever reach out to again.

Tune into those valuable assets you notice about the people you encounter, and factor them into your marketing strategy equation.

> *"Honor those little voices, hunches, intuition that tell you what to do. Because over your whole life, you've built experience, character, integrity. Your personal brand is what you stand for. Trust those hunches."*
> —**Mary Ann Pierce,** *Founder and CEO at MAP Digital*[30]

3) Organize and systematize to keep you on track with ease.

- **You don't have to remember it all.** Use a CRM to keep contact information including your personal notes about the people in your sphere (this works great for current clients as well). Note birthdays and personal events like weddings or speaking gigs. Before you get on a call, glance at your notes so you can include something personal in your conversation.

- *Make it a team effort.* If you want your sales team to use this strategy, give them the systems support they need. Encourage them to confer with each other on their lists, strategies, content, etc. Cross-fertilizing communication can be game-changing.
- *Employ the contact that never gets old*: hand-written cards or gifts. Everyone loves to receive something in the mail! Create a simple, easy system to send a gift or card as a special touchpoint. My tradition is to gift the important people in my Transformational Ties community with a small token of my regard each year during the holiday season (tip: I start early to organize).

Your goal: to regularly keep in touch with your connections in a way that's personal and authentic, supported by a system that embeds your communication approach in your personal "culture." Even better, expand this practice as part of the company's organizational culture, as an ingredient of a responsive and compassionate brand – as well as a sales generator!

How to make your people rainmakers for seven-figure success

Yes, I mean ALL your people, not just your sales team and leadership stars! If you've brought together the best of the best, moving forward together toward the company's vision, then why not enroll them in making meaningful contacts and developing Transformational Ties that will make selling a breeze?

In too many companies, teams/departments become silos where sales doesn't talk to marketing, marketing doesn't talk to R&D, no one talks to the receptionists or frontline customer service people – you get the idea.

A rainmaker is a term often used to describe a person who's not just a salesperson but has a knack for generating new business – win a contract, close warm leads, find nontraditional ways to bring on prospective customers, develop long-term lucrative opportunities. This is my view:

Everyone can help make rain to produce a great harvest.

Through their personal engagement, initiative, and the relationships they build on behalf of the company, each of your people can be planting the seeds for future business.

The key is to create a culture that has ALL team members out there representing the company they are proud to be part of.

"I encourage my people to join community programs and speak at churches, synagogues, Girl Scouts, you name it. We start by seeing what their interests and passions are, then match their message with whatever group they are, or want to be, associated with. To me it's the best way to develop business." ~Michele Mirman, Senior Partner and Founder, Mirman, Markovits & Landau, P.C.[31]

The challenge is that few professional services firms are set up to collaborate, mentor, and train in this way. Everybody's working on their book of business which lends itself to a competitive rather than collaborative environment.

I love the example of a woman I admire, Barbara Yong, Partner at Golan Christie Taglia LLP. She defied the odds in her law firm by promoting a collaborative culture that actually increased business, retained talented employees and partners, and earned the firm the reputation as a great place to work!

"We created a culture where we helped each other by taking on each other's clients, which allowed us all to collaborate and have a say in our culture. We made space to hire young attorneys and help them grow. We trained them, empowered them, and taught them how to be their own business generators. So, people felt like they were a valuable part of the firm – and they were," says, Barbara Yong. "For me it was investing not only in the business but in each other's success." [32]

Visionary Action Step # 2:
Give your people the resources they need to learn about and represent your company.

- ***Help your people learn about the business*** – how it runs, who its clients are, what others' roles and responsibilities are, etc. (Remember the Four Seasons model of onboarding and training every employee?) Encourage your managers/team leads to initiate ways to engage their reports on all levels, and keep their "office doors" open to questions and feedback.
- ***Find ways to get everyone to the table***. The best companies value the unique contributions of their people. I for one always turn to my team on topics where they're stronger than I am – I learn so much from their expertise. I can't imagine trying to do this by myself. More importantly, it educates and empowers them to be active partners in representing and promoting my company.
- ***Give them the resources to pursue their own Transformational Ties.*** Make your tech and admin systems available to everyone so they have what they need to be effective, valuable rainmakers for your company.

Sell like a Visionary Leader by nailing the "Solution Conversation"

So, you have built a Transformational Tie with someone and now you're in the place of doing business with them and closing that deal. I've done many presentations and run programs where I teach the concept of sales conversations – however I don't call them that: ***"Solution conversations" are the secret to successful conversion, especially at the seven-figure level.***

Solution Conversations come out of this mindset: ***Rather than get them to buy, find out how to help them.*** In these conversations, you and the potential customer are working together to identify their problems and work out possible solutions.

"My motivation is just providing great service to our clients and helping them grow...but also making a difference in the world. If you provide value in your service and you make a difference for people, the money will come – I not only truly believe this, I've experienced it firsthand."
—**Corey S. Kupfer,** *Owner of Kupfer & Associates PLLC*[33]

Before most sales conversations, imagine the thoughts that often turn over and over in our minds: *What if I blow this deal? Should I try to get more out of them – or settle for less? This deal's going to put me over my sales goals for this quarter – and buy my next car! Whew, so much pressure!*

Now think about coming from the service mindset that Corey describes. Then follow these five steps to a Solution Conversation that will convert your connection to a loyal and lucrative client:

1) Listen more than you speak. Pay attention and be present. The best communicators are actually great listeners, even in a business sales and negotiation conversation. It's important because you're about to ask for a commitment from them to trust you to meet their most urgent needs, and to lay down some big dollars to do so.

- Listen with curiosity. Open your heart. Open your mind. Open up to your sincere interest in them, their needs and the roadblocks they may be facing.
- Listen not only through your ears, but also with your eyes, your gut and your heart. Listen for what is being said, as well as what is NOT being said. Body language and personality come into play and combine for a wallop impact.

2) Identify the problems of your potential client. As you ask questions, reflect back to them what you're hearing and methodically lay out the problems. This technique allows you to make sure you understand what they want, and offers them the chance to get everything out on the table.

Then determine how the work you will do with them is their solution, tying your value to the problems they've outlined. Keep it focused on them, *not your methodology.* They want to know and believe that you WILL be able to solve their problems or meet their intended outcomes, not your particular backstory of the HOW (at least at this point in the process).

3) Craft a proposal with a scope of work that fits the client's exact needs. The scope conversation is extremely important because you are working together to ensure:

- You are going to fit the client's need.
- They trust that you are the ones to meet that need.
- They help co-create the scope so there are no surprises once they are presented with the proposal.

Remember, for high price-point engagements, boilerplate doesn't work – don't fall into that one-size-fits-all trap if you want the competitive edge.

Give them a basic overview of what solving their problem will look like for them, then fill in with the specifics of the engagement you are proposing. Consider the "trust" piece as you describe the ways you are going to take care of them *at every step of the engagement.* Make sure you are being *clear about the scope of what you CAN do as well as what is NOT part of the engagement (you don't need to go into details here yet you want to be* clear *about important parameters).*

Remember, the client is likely interviewing other potential people to hire, so you want them to see why *you* are the one they need.

I am a firm believer that **when I present a proposal there should be NO surprises – because the unexpected can stop a sale in its tracks.** The way to avoid this issue is to work closely and clearly with the potential client so that you are co-creating the scope. They are all-in with the process, hence no surprises.

4) Schedule a conversation to walk through the proposal together.
DO NOT follow up by emailing them a proposal. In so doing, you often find yourself steeped in playing the "chase the client" game (maybe this sounds familiar?).

Instead, schedule a video conference or live meeting with them to present your proposal. Then walk them through it: You read it through with them, referencing their problems and pain points from the earlier conversations that brought you to this potential engagement, and explaining how this specific proposal is going to support them.

Important: **Stand your ground to represent you, your brand, your company, and your belief in your ability to deliver what this client needs. Call up your 17X confidence – no waffling!**

Now, ask for their response, and, again, put all your levels of listening skills in play so you are answering their questions correctly and providing the specifics they want to hear.

At the conclusion of the meeting, I always ask what else they need to know to make a decision and move forward. If they are talking to other companies, I ask what their timeline will be to make their decision.

I do my best to schedule the next meeting AT THAT MOMENT before we part.

5) Follow up. This is the final piece to the sales puzzle and the toughest one to navigate. You don't want to leave a proposal with them and then just hang around waiting for a response.

How often do you follow up? What type of follow-up methods do you use?

There are no right or wrong answers here. It's personal and specific to that potential client and to your business. Because you know them so well at this point, trust yourself to know the right way to approach them in a way that will resonate.

Follow-up usually involves addressing their concerns and hesitations (and sometimes fears), so it could be helpful to include in your follow-up the invitation to address those concerns.

One thing I can say for sure is that if you don't follow up, you will lose the sale. 100%.

Finally, remember, the answer is not always a *no*. It may be a *not yet, not ready* (maybe taking the "tortoise" approach), or *not now*. Remember, this response can change in a day, weeks, a month or maybe years, so hang in there. If you are the right choice, the sale will close. The key here is the long-term game...staying in touch.

Trust it.

Seven-Figure Selling: TAKEAWAYS

Playing the long game: Taking your time with rapid growth.

- Take your time to find, grow and nurture the Transformational Ties that build a flow of business that will increase your sales exponentially.
- Consider building connections as an integral part of your marketing strategy, and support it as such.
- Identify and make a list of your connections to launch the strategic process.
- Make building Transformational Ties a team effort!

Three visionary steps to make your people rainmakers

- Give your people the resources to learn about the business so they can represent the company

- Find ways to get everyone to the table – empower them to contribute from their expertise.
- Make the tech and admin systems available to everyone so they have what they need to be effective rainmakers for your business.

Sell like a *Visionary Leader* by nailing the Solution Conversation.

- Follow the five steps to a Solution Conversation that will convert your connection to a loyal and lucrative client.

    » *Listen more than you speak. Pay attention and be present.*
    » *Identify the problems of your potential client.*
    » *Craft a proposal with a scope of work that fits the client's exact needs.*
    » *Schedule a conversation to walk through the proposal together.*
    » Follow up! Trust the process!

SOLUTION CONVERSATION CHEATSHEET

INSTRUCTIONS: Use this as a reminder and support, to take notes in preparation, and track how you did, what to celebrate, and what to improve upon.

1.   Listen more than I speak. Pay attention and be present. Ask curious questions to learn as much as I can about them and their needs.

_____

_____

_____

2.   What are this potential client's problems to solve?

_____

_____

_____

3.   How will the work I do provide them with their solution? Keep focused on them, not our methodology.

_____

_____

_____

4. Craft a proposal with a scope of work that fits the client's exact needs to ensure:

    -   I am going to fit the client's needs. Talking points:

    _____

    _____

    _____

    -   They trust us to be the ones to meet that need. Talking points:

    _____

    _____

    _____

    -   They help co-create the scope so there are no surprises once they are presented with the proposal. Talking points:

    _____

    _____

    _____

5. Conversation scheduled to walk through proposal: I'm standing my ground to represent me, my brand, company, and believe in my ability to deliver what this client needs!

    _____

    _____

    _____

6. Ask for their response, answer their questions correctly, and address specifics and concerns.

_____

_____

_____

7. At the end, ask: "What else do you need to know to make a decision and move forward?" Ask what their timeline will be to make their decision. Try to schedule the next meeting AT THAT MOMENT before we part.

_____

_____

_____

8. Follow up! Respectfully keep in contact. Address further concerns and hesitations. Keep their interests in mind.

_____

_____

_____

Remember, the answer is not always a no. It may be a not yet, not ready, or not now. This response can change in a day, weeks, a month, or maybe years. If I am the right choice, the sale will close. The key here is the long-term game...staying in touch. Trust it.

CHAPTER NINE

THE NEW STANDARD FOR EXTRAORDINARY

"The way to ensure that you become a good leader is to – every chance you get – reflect upon your chosen path, make sure you are on it, and remind yourself of the reasons you are on it. Let it settle in your heart and do not look back."

—**Joe Curcillo,** Strategic Advisor at
Generalist's Advantage Strategies LTD

hen we are at our best, our companies are at their best. Am I right?

When you marry the inner work and outer actions we've covered in these chapters so far, you are positioning yourself to join the ranks of the best of the best. To recap:

- Unleashing your Inner Visionary and tapping into your personal power
- Working with the power of pure profit to take control of your numbers
- Becoming that legacy-making influencer who brings people together to get things done
- 17X-ing your confidence to BE the Visionary Leader you know you can be, and to take visionary actions for your business and your life

- Building multi-million dollar magic through your Business Growth Game Plan and can-do culture
- Attracting, hiring, positioning and empowering your best-of-the-best team
- Looking ahead with visionary marketing for tomorrow's market needs
- Mastering seven-figure selling through Transformational Ties, rainmakers and Solutions Conversations

I know that you could stop here, use this information, do these worksheets, and be VERY happy with the significant new levels of rapid growth and leadership success you will realize.

Yet there's more that I want for you!

Evolving a better version of yourself as a Visionary Leader

This is what I've seen in my own life and in the clients I work with: ***To be at the top of your game you must be continuously working on yourself.*** If you are not at your physical and mental best, you won't see the magic of the elements in your business coming together and moving forward toward the sales and success you deserve.

Are you ready? Then let's talk about three keys to evolving yourself as a Visionary Leader:

1. **Show up regularly as your best possible self**

2. **Prepare yourself for maximum extraordinary visibility**

3. **Let your BIG BOLD VISION lead the way to extraordinary results**

1. Show up regularly as your best possible self

So, what does showing up as your best self look like?

You see it when you watch the sports greats, celebrated artists and top-performing celebrities who bring it *every single time* to the best of their ability.

We're inspired by excellence. We cheer on the people who make it big through facing setbacks and challenges. Before building a legacy company and winning 22 Academy Awards, Walt Disney was fired from one of his first animation jobs because he "lacked imagination and had no good ideas," according to *The Wisdom of Oz: Using Personal Accountability to Succeed in Everything You Do,* by Roger Conners and Tom Smith.[34] J.K. Rowling got fired because she was secretly writing her stories at work and you know the rest: She went on to write one of the most successful book series of all time about a wizard named Harry Potter.

It's no different in business leadership – that is, if you want to reach a standard of extraordinary rather than just coast through life on autopilot!

You want to be at your best, continuing to show up, all-in, all the time. Even – especially – when it feels hopeless. Even when you don't make it to the finals or get the Grammy or nail the promotion. Even when your plans don't happen as expected.

How many times have you lost out on a big contract or not hit your revenue goals? Maybe something completely out of your control happened – a speaking gig cancellation, a flight delay, a team member leaving unexpectedly, a health flare-up that set you back, a global pandemic...

How do Visionary Leaders do it?

Visionary Action Step #1:
Remember why you're in this.

In my many years as a business owner, I have "quit" numerous times – truth! I suspect at some point we've all proclaimed, "I'm done!" And then we show up again the very next day, recalibrated and ready to go. Why is that?

I believe that if you're in the right business or career for you, then your work has meaning and makes a difference in the world. You have the ability to change people's lives – your clients, customers, partners, employees, community, and someone across the globe you've never even met. It's this meaning that carries you through those moments of "I'm done!"

That's how it is for me with Slater Success: As long as I have breath and energy, I am here for it. My drive is sustained by my clients' successes. They completely thrill me and I love being a part of their story. Are there ups and downs? Sure. It's the bigger purpose that carries me through the downs and celebrates the ups.

I'm sure love of the work and its meaning is what drives all the greats to become the extraordinary stars we respect and adore.

1) *Take some time to think about and celebrate your great fortune to be doing what you love!* Reflect on the following questions. And if you currently are NOT doing what you love, it's an even better time to answer these questions, and take lessons from the answers to help you find more fulfilling work:

- *Why am I in this business?*
- *What meaning does my current work have for me?*
- *What do I love about the work I do?*

Write down your answers to see them in black-and-white and embed them in your brain.

Bonus question: ***Are you building your business from a place of joy?*** When you do, you can accomplish anything. If you are not, chances are you're not being your best, and perhaps missing opportunities for growth.

It very much comes down to mindset, and if you can't answer this question with a full-throated YES, then it's important for you to explore why, and to consider ways that you could feel more joy in your work.

2) *Help yourself remember why you do what you do, to get you through those times when you've forgotten.* Even the best of the best have the worst days. When you are faced with setbacks that challenge your comfort zone, have you questioning your worth or just make you want to throw in the towel, do things that can remind you of why you're in this and that can help you snap back into positivity, clarity and focus. Then you move forward again.

> *"There's not one crisis we have been through (Hurricane Sandy was a big one for me) that hasn't made us smarter and stronger."*
> —**Stacy Francis,** *CEO of Francis Financial and Founder of Savvy Ladies*[35]

Here are some suggestions to help you through the setbacks and questioning:

- An easy start: Do or review the **Top 10 Things Technique** from Chapter Four.
- Create different practices that will take you out of stuckness and clear your head. We all have different and favorite methods... such as:
  - » A round of golf with friends
  - » A walk in nature
  - » Conversation with a dear friend or colleague who listens well and holds space for you to download where you are
  - » Listening to music by yourself for an hour
  - » Moving your body through running, exercise, dancing, biking, yoga, etc.
  - » Doing something creative with your hands like playing guitar, construction, gardening, painting

Regular self-care helps you get back on your feet more quickly when you hit obstacles. We often think that these activities are a luxury or an extra-curricular option. **For the Visionary Leader, self-care is non-negotiable!**

- Simply getting away can be a great disruptor. Remove yourself from whatever is sapping your energy and motivation, whether it's for a few days or a few weeks. Gaining some distance from the problems and clearing your head can be just the ticket to come back stronger than ever.

Prepare yourself for maximum extraordinary visibility

It's probably obvious we will never be visible by clinging to the walls trying to blend in with the wallpaper at networking events. What's not so obvious is that visibility is a BIG deal that can bring fame and fortune – and also blindside you in ways you never anticipated.

It takes preparation to be extraordinarily successful. I'll show you what I mean...

Ivy's Office Hours: I'd been working with my client, Peter, on ways to expand his brand visibility. Sure enough, he posted a blog that attracted a New York Times journalist, who asked him to contribute as an expert for a news story. The article was published, and I encouraged him to do some promotion around it on social media. He did and the response was astonishing – thousands of comments and shares in the first 24 hours, and continuing for weeks thereafter!

Naturally, Peter's inbox started showing regular messages, like "I read you in the New York Times," "Spot-on comment in the news," and "Let's get together for coffee; there are some things I'd love to get your help on..."

Awesome, right? In our next coaching call, I asked how it was going.

Peter: *It's been great but overwhelming. A week ago, it just felt like too much....so I shut down all social media and haven't posted since.*

Me: *Oh?* Inside I'm screaming: *What – shut down your media? Isn't this what we planned for, what you dreamed of happening?*

I decided it was time to get to the bottom of what this was really about: *Peter, how did you feel when this article first hit?*

Peter: *I felt really good.*

Me: *So...when did that change?*

Peter: *I just started feeling awkward and weird when all these people kept emailing me and commenting.*

Me: *It sounds to me like they were looking to you as a leader. And maybe you aren't seeing yourself that way. Could that be true – and why you pulled back?*

Peter paused: *Oh...one hundred percent. I see what happened – and now I just shot myself in the foot..."*

Then he backpedaled: *Well, you know it was just one article; it's not like I'm an expert or pundit or have any chance of converting all those commenters into clients...* And so on.

We went on to talk about how he never thought he lacked self-confidence until he had to look in the mirror and own that he was a leader. I pointed out to him that he IS in fact a leader. He CAN in fact follow up with these people, some of whom will hire him. And it's likely he WILL be approached by someone or produce something again that will get a huge response.

Then I asked the money questions: *Do you want to grow your business? Do you want to grow as a professional and an expert in your field? Do you want to help more people?*

Peter: *Yes, I do!*

Me: You acknowledge that the content you put out there is important and of value, right? (Peter nodded.) So, all of that – everything you do in your work – is YOU. That's your brand and that is what all those people are attracted to. Let me tell you, you deserve it.

So, Peter, if this is true and you want to grow your business…then you must find a way to feel comfortable being visible, to own the extraordinary leader that you are!

In addition to getting back on track with his social media marketing, Peter stepped into ownership of his Visionary Leadership by taking an action that was really outside his comfort zone and would expand his business exponentially. Now he could imagine the extraordinary – and he reaped the rewards for his action.

If you believe that visibility pushes your comfort zone, you may want to answer some of the questions I would ask a client like Peter:

- *What would happen if my business had more visibility?*
- *In what ways could my business reach more people and get more profitable?*
- *What steps can I take to increase that visibility to meet those kinds of goals? How far am I willing to go?*

Many of us would give our right arm for the sake of our business and our people, but not so much for our own sakes. It's understandable to shy away from the spotlight, and prefer to just focus on the work you do and take care of your clients and employees.

The truth is, that's not enough.

If you want sales success and legacy greatness, you have to market your business. In order to market it, you must be visible.

Start by taking small steps outside your comfort zone (We've talked about this already in regard to boosting confidence – same principle), little by little, to meet those goals you've just outlined that would improve your business's visibility. Each step will lead to more success and confidence **_until visibility becomes part of who you are as a Visionary Leader._**

Now, you might already own your leadership and welcome opportunities to be visible – that's great! Keep stepping up, and work on your personal branding.

Visionary Action Step #2:
Expect success. Prepare for extraordinary.

The main reason Peter was so taken aback from his visibility going viral is that he didn't expect it.

If you are planning a campaign to gain visibility, then also plan for its success!

Once you push _send_ on a blog article or podcast, once you sit on a televised expert panel or speak to a large audience – it's out there reaching distances beyond what you could imagine or control. These are scary moments, no doubt, and you can't predict what kind of responses are going to come back.

However, you CAN prepare for and leverage the outcomes. Take actions to manage your experience and protect your boundaries, your time, and the company's investment.

And while others are coasting on autopilot, keeping safe and silent, YOU are living your own standards of extraordinary, out there meeting your public with power, authenticity, and legacy-making influence, having the time of your life!

**1) To support yourself emotionally** through your experience:

- Pull out all the stops on your 17X-ed confidence.
- Do not engage in Imposter Syndrome.
- Engage a personal coach or therapist.
- Step up your self-care regimen.
- Bring your "kitchen cabinet" and cheerleaders in close.

2) *Prepare in advance to handle the responses* when branding/marketing goes viral (and also when it doesn't and the only response is "crickets"):

- Mentally prepare for responses by creating messaging that you can have ready when you need it. This way you won't get blindsided by a sudden call from a journalist who wants a quick quote from you. Get ready also for no response at all by having a Plan B on hand to uplevel or adjust your communication.
- Delegate responsibilities like tracking responses, building your CRM, managing your online social media accounts, doing initial follow-ups, and running interference for you.
- Enlist the help of your team or engage an assistant to take over and automate processes.

Your people can't always stand in for you, of course, but delegating opens up space for you to show up at your best without stress or overwhelm. Allow emerging rainmakers and leaders to take part as company/brand ambassadors – you gain more time and space, and they gain a great growth opportunity.

Let your Big Bold Vision lead the way to extraordinary

Many people do their company vision and goals in the fall for the following year – and never visit them again until the next fall. They don't have a process in place to revisit them during the year; they don't use them as a foundation for working regularly with their numbers.

I understand why and I don't hold it against them! As I've said before, we are busy just running our company or leading the department day-to-day. It can be a challenge to make the time to do much more than what's continually calling our attention.

Here's the problem: The vision is there somewhere, a cloudy North Star we see faintly and follow...sometimes. We don't stop to manage it, adapt it or ***make it extraordinary.*** We stay in our risk-averse comfort zone...and wonder why we're not expanding, scaling, growing, having the impact we want (or feeling the joy).

Trust me, that's NOT what the best of the best are doing!

Remember your **Big Bold Vision** in Chapter Five? Here's where it comes to the rescue – a powerful tool that has you asking these questions, then exploring the answers, vetting new possibilities, setting the direction to achieve them, and using this roadmap to all things extraordinary:

- *Is my vision being all it can be?*
- *What if I took this further?*
- *What does the best of the best look like for me?*
- *What can I do to get there?*

I love taking my clients through this process so they can stretch their imaginations and see possibilities they hadn't thought of before – things that will help them grow and scale their business, set up a secure financial future, and identify a lifestyle they would love to have. Some people might call it stretch goals or dreams. Whatever you call it, please do the process AND the follow-up.

Ivy's Office Hours: Tonya was founder and head of an established boutique firm with a steady stream of revenue and an up-marketed client base. She was in her 50's, with two adult children. She came to me to work on sustaining growth, succession and legacy planning for her business. She was about to get more than she'd bargained for – in the best possible way!

Tonya was surprised by my question: *What do you want your life and business to look like in ten years?*

She struggled for a while, then finally: *I don't know exactly what I want, I can't predict the future. Is something wrong here? Why am I doing this work if I can't picture where it's all going to take me?*

So, I took her through a series of questions to help her imagine what she might want to HAVE and BE in the future (part of the Alignment

Process I described in Chapter Four). Helping nudge along her imagination, which she admitted she hadn't done in a long time, we discovered together that she:

- Loves being in New York and Miami, and it would be a dream to have a second, or third, home in one of those cities.
- Wants to be able to travel to see her kids and grandkids regularly – in fact how cool would it be to own a property like a compound where they all could gather for vacation?
- Would like to be financially secure enough to build out a trust for whatever grandchildren came along.
- Has a deep interest in working with domestic violence issues, and would like more time to volunteer, and maybe serve on a board.

We explored several creative options and choices Tonya could make to move herself toward realizing these dreams – her Big Bold Vision.

In our next strategy call, we explored some scenarios and started some planning, looking more specifically at goals and the financial pieces she could put in place right now.

Visionary Action Step #3:
Explore the Big Bold Vision of your
professional and personal future.

Your Big Bold Vision is likely outside your comfort zone or beyond what you can imagine right now, whether it's because you are too busy, you doubt you can create the future you dream of, haven't exercised your Inner Visionary muscle, or just haven't thought that far ahead yet.

Let me tell you that, no matter what your age, NOW is the time to start creating the future you want to live in.

Until I took her there, Tonya had never entertained the idea of blending her business goals with a vision for her future. Her Big Bold Vision now informs all her business and personal decisions, and she is excited about the future she's in the process of creating.

Go there! Explore what you want for yourself and your business in 5-10 years. Do the exploration alone, with a coach, consultant, confidant, or significant other.

Follow these four steps:

1) Keep in mind your overall vision that's been uncovered by your Inner Visionary. Call it up again as your North Star. Tap into your imagination and allow yourself to see it happening.

2) Ask yourself questions like the following, imagining what's possible to have in your future years AND what you believe will be important to you in that future. Get your answers in writing so you can play with the possibilities:

- *What do I love about my life?*
- *Do I picture M&A, selling my company, succession, retirement? If so, what does that look like?*
- *Where do I imagine living in five years from now? Ten years?*
- *How do I picture my family life in 5 – 10 years?*
- *What things give me meaning in my life that I want to start or continue doing (like creative activities, athletics, social activism, political involvement, love of animals, gaming, museums, travel, etc.)*

3) Sort out your priorities, options, and goals around these answers. Then set it all down as a plan.

Important note: You don't have to know the "how" yet. Counterintuitive? Not really. You are setting things in place as best you can for a future you cannot predict. So, don't try to figure it all out or you'll just stress out. Trust that you are putting in place actions to work toward what is (and probably always will be) most important for you.

Even as you change or tweak along the way, even as life and business throw you curveballs, you will still be in alignment with your Inner Visionary which houses your core beliefs, desires, and dreams—with these, you can't stray far.

4) Keep your Big Bold Vision alive by incorporating it into your business, personal and financial plans.

Each quarter, I meet with every one of my clients to look at what has been accomplished in the previous quarter, and what we are setting up for the next. We cover all financial areas of the business:

- Marketing
- Sales
- Operations
- Strategic plans for growth and scaling
- Big Bold Vision plans

When you assess each ending quarter, do your numbers to make sure they align, then adjust the next quarter accordingly. And include your Big Bold Vision in the assessment. Ask:

- *What have I accomplished? What's working? What is not?*
- *What needs to be adjusted from the last quarter, in terms of goals and numbers?*
- *What do I need to shift or change in this year's goals in response to the vision I set for the year?*
- *Am I on track to move toward what I really want? If not, what must I change or shift?*

The inner work is owning and believing that you can do what's in the Big Bold Vision you have created. The outer actions are to do the numbers, create your Business Growth Game Plan, and take action steps toward achieving that vision.

This is how you set your new standard for extraordinary in your business and personal life. Everything is creatable. It's yours to create.

Visionary Action Step #4:
Run your business today with a vision for tomorrow.

Fortified with your Big Bold Vision, you will be better prepared for those curveballs and times that will test your confidence and competence (because they WILL occur).

> *"I believe you can develop the muscle, the sort of sensory memory, which gives you the instinctual ability and confidence to manage through chaos and crisis. And know that it's an expertise you'll have and that you can rely on in the future."*
> **—Beth Haggerty,**
> *Executive, Entrepreneur, Board Member, Advisor*[36]

How does the Visionary Leader make plans when the future is so unpredictable?

Here are five steps to extraordinary leadership during both good times and bad times:

1. **Communication is key**: Listen with your eyes, ears, heart and gut in order to get the whole picture, so you don't leave out departments or experts who might have the exact perspective or solution you need.

2. **Know the strengths of your people** and how to use those strengths as a resource. Form a top-tier team and trust in them. You need people to delegate to, brainstorm with, rely on, and have on your (and the company's) side.

3. **Use the external environment**, your customers and the marketplace to guide you in decisions to pivot and adapt. Don't circle your wagons and miss opportunities.

4. ***Be a strong decision maker***: Balance your *tortoise and hare* aspects; assess your options; and make the best decision you can at the time knowing you have the ability to course correct. Waffling or making no decision at all stops all growth, for not just the leader and the team but the entire business.

5. ***Keep connecting***, building, enhancing and nurturing old and new Transformational Ties. When you have those moments of needing to pull together a support team or resources, you'll have these relationships at your fingertips.

    Transformational Ties also give you the power to connect other people to one another and be a catalyst for introductions. This is more valuable than you'll ever be able to measure, in good times as well as challenging times.

The New Standard
for Extraordinary:
TAKEAWAYS

When you're at your best, your company's at its best (and your life is at its best).

To be at the top of your game you must continually work on yourself. If you aren't, you won't see the magic of the elements of your business coming together toward the sales and success you desire. Three keys to evolving yourself as a Visionary Leader:

Show up regularly as your best possible self so your company can be at its best.

- Take some time to think about and celebrate your great fortune to be doing what you love!

- Help yourself remember why you do what you do, to get you through those times when you've forgotten.

Prepare yourself for maximum extraordinary visibility.

- To support yourself emotionally, exercise self-care and gather support.
- Expect success. Prepare in advance to handle responses when branding/marketing goes viral.

Let your Big Bold Vision lead the way to your own new standard of extraordinary.

- Explore the Big Bold Vision of your professional and personal future by opening your mind and asking yourself questions about what it will/could look like.
- Run your business for today as the Big Bold Vision you see it being in the future.

BIG BOLD VISION WORKSHEET

INSTRUCTIONS: Ready to step outside your comfort zone? OK! Explore what you want for yourself and your business in 5-10 years. Tapping into your Inner Visionary, explore these questions:

1. What do I love about my life?

   _____

   _____

   _____

2. Where do I imagine living 5 years from now? Ten years?

   _____

   _____

   _____

3. How do I picture my family life in 5 - 10 years?

   _____

   _____

   _____

4. Do I picture M&A, selling my company, succession, or retirement? If so, what does that look like?

_____

_____

_____

5. What things give me meaning in my life that I want to start or continue doing (like creative activities, athletics, social activism, political involvement, love of animals, gaming, museums, travel, etc.)

_____

_____

_____

Now, take a breath, walk around the block, and answer this set of questions, to help incorporate your BBV into your business and financial plans:

1. What have I accomplished? What's working? What is not?

_____

_____

_____

2. What needs to be adjusted from the last quarter, in terms of goals and numbers?

   _____

   _____

   _____

3. What do I need to shift or change in this year's goals in response to the vision I set for the year?

   _____

   _____

   _____

4. Am I on track to move toward what I really want? If not, what must I change or shift?

   _____

   _____

   _____

Do the numbers, and create/update your Business Growth Game Plan.

CHAPTER TEN

THE ULTIMATE EVOLUTION OF YOU AND YOUR COMPANY

"Every day, I have the privilege of meeting entrepreneurs and founders to gain an understanding of their business, their vision and the legacy they want to leave, with the goal of helping to facilitate building a strategically significant business."

—**Maurissa Bell,** Private Equity Investor[37]

ome business owners think succession planning doesn't happen until you're looking to exit your business.

I don't necessarily agree with that. ***I believe that – right now – planning for your exit can be the catalyst to move your business forward!***

I was talking to a client recently who said, "You know, I'm not quite sure about the next few years – what does 'exit' look like and am I going to exit? What's best for me? What's best for the company?"

We started looking at what her plans were for the future, and decided that the next couple of years our focus would be on EBITDA – the company's overall financial performance and its growth strategy – to move her business forward as well as to set the company on the path of positioning for an eventual exit.

Often succession planning and strategic planning go hand in hand. They both are essential to building a healthy, solid, thriving business.

What distinguishes the best of the best from the average leader is how they take their next steps to the future. As we know, the Visionary Leader keeps their eye on the horizon, the influence and impact they want to make on the world, and the legacy they want to leave behind.

However, it's natural for us to be so busy with our current business and personal lives that we don't think about the next evolutionary steps to take until it becomes important – or back-against-the-wall crucial – to do so in our later years.

If you have not given this any thought or if you don't have a vision for the future of your business, then I say, *Get on it! It's time!* It doesn't matter if you're thirty, forty, fifty, sixty or seventy.

Thinking in legacy terms *now* sets you on a course of intentionally and actively **building your company through the lens of the future!** Your vision, strategic plans, decisions and actions guide you steadily toward creating your future life.

A lot can be accomplished by implementing the two-to-five-year plans I've described in this book. Visualizing and planning the *evolution* of your company is a bigger, longer-term endeavor. It can be exciting, yet daunting, to take your company to that next level.

This is why I'm going to share some considerations with you that I hope will smooth your path.

Three keys to "evolutionizing" your company

Look at it this way: **What you plant today you will reap tomorrow.**

Whatever the ultimate evolution of your business becomes, it starts with positioning your company in terms of market relevance, profitability, governance, and growth potential – all the areas we have been covering in this book – while always aligning with your vision.

What does this look like?

> **Key #1: Scale your company for greater profitability**
>
> **Key #2: Prepare you and your company for the next (BOLD) iteration**
>
> **Key #3: Make the next-level moves – creating your exit and your legacy**

KEY #1:
SCALE YOUR COMPANY FOR GREATER PROFITABILITY.

Many think that growing your business is the same as scaling. There is one key difference. **When you're growing a business**, you are adding revenue at the same pace that you are adding resources such as staff, new equipment and tech, marketing and branding.

When you're scaling a business, you are adding revenue at a much higher rate than cost through strategic investing. You are playing in a whole new ball field. You are building capacity beyond just keeping pace with your current model. You are multiplying your successes, whether it's more products, more locations, more markets, or more influence.

Why do you want to scale? From clients I've worked with over the years, I see three main reasons:

- To expand operations (locations, services, customers, leadership, etc.).
- To meet a new market need or opportunity.
- To eventually sell the business or retire and pass on their book of business.

Visionary Action Step #1:
Take these steps for successful scaling.

1) *Your vision should be limitless.* Over time as you grow and change and your business grows and changes, your vision can and should shift. The first plan you put to paper is rarely the one that ends up coming through in the end. As you implement your initial plans, you get continued insights on where your vision and strategy meet, and then you make adjustments and welcome the shifts. That's where real success happens!

As I've shared earlier, my vision when I started Slater Success has changed over time.

I have found my sweet spot (at least for now!) where I feel I make a meaningful impact as well as profit, working with both women and men in professional services, most of whom are founders and/or CEOs.

My Big Bold Vision essentially hasn't changed nor have my core values or personal goals; however, the work I am doing now was not in the original Business Growth Game Plan I came up with back in 2008.

As for my clients, many have built their businesses and reached new revenue milestones, where they experience opportunities for funding and expansion they hadn't anticipated in the timeline of their vision. Exciting!

2) *Keep up with your plan with a triple-A method: ASSESS, ANALYZE, ADJUST.* Scaling a business means new directions, big decisions, bigger risk, big-time gains, and more money than you perhaps (and hopefully!) have ever dealt with before. Regularly keeping track of the moving parts and staying on track are crucial to success in scaling.

- ***Make sure your plan is working for YOU*** (not what other companies may be doing) and that it covers those moving parts: marketing, sales, money, team, operations and mindset.
- ***Regularly look at your financial plan***. As you'll see later, keeping up with your numbers is especially important if you are considering raising capital in a private equity (PE), venture capital (VC) or other investor situation, because you're going to need to report.
- ***Be bold, make a plan, take action*** – and do that over and over again. Once you set a goal, keep moving until you reach it or reach a version of it, and then make a new plan. Keep at it, and you'll get there!

3) Scale your team: Bring in new people while preserving your culture. Hire the support you need when you're ready to scale, NOT once your business is already starting to grow.

- ***Reverse engineer your hiring.*** Simply adding on people as you discover the need isn't going to build the team you need for the future. Take these steps to build your dream team:
  - » Consider what kinds of skills, etc. would be an asset to your vision and plan.
  - » Put your essential systems in place to support your plan.
  - » Staff with the appropriate people/teams you currently have, shifting roles, making promotions, designating leaders, etc.
  - » Do the hiring for the new skills and support you'll need to create that future.

Alex Simpson is Co-founder and Chair of Liquid LP, a business which focuses on enabling limited partners and general partners with lending solutions. He is also an advisor and investor in various fintech companies. When Alex looks at a company, a standout characteristic for him is the leadership culture. He believes the biggest asset of a company is its employees. "A sense of loyalty is really important. I look at retention rates, longevity and how strong the culture is." [38]

- ***Training is an investment: ensure your team is onboard and ready to go***: You want everyone to move forward together. This means thorough training, open lines of communication, and delegating to your current people the opportunity and responsibility to mentor the new hires.

  » Have good training principles in place, including a Standard Operating Procedures (SOP) manual (types of manuals might include print, video recording or clips to meet all types of learning).

  » In designing your training – and expected outcomes – keep in mind that once you hire it can take three to six months to get a new team member up to speed.

  » Does this feel like a heavy lift? Then consider this: The average cost to replace a team member in a professional services firm is equivalent to that position's one-year salary (taking into account not just rehiring but the indirect costs of lost productivity and bringing them up to speed). The importance of putting time and energy into training your current team is invaluable.

- ***Prepare to tweak and make changes in the early days.*** The truth is that not all your initial systems, processes, and hires are going to work perfectly.

  » Again, regularly assess, analyze, and adjust. In terms of systems, you may consider "dating before marriage" with a provisional contract, or leasing instead of purchasing equipment.

  » Address errors early on – and make thoughtful decisions around your people and teams, always with clear communication and transparency.

  » The old adage is true here: Hire slow, fire fast – using a methodical hiring process that ensures good decision making and due diligence.

  » Test the winds and make adjustments that will move you forward.

Once again, your people and your relationships are everything! If someone shows they are not a good fit for your particular situation, let them go and help them with their next steps. (There have been people I've let go who wrote me thank-you notes later because they made a better move!)

Ariana J. Tadler, founding partner of Tadler Law LLP, tells me how she takes the pulse of her firm by enlisting input from her team: "We encourage everybody at the firm to help us make sure we're on track: *What are we doing right? What are we doing wrong? How can we do better? Is there something weighing on you that I'm not aware of?* I really aim to be responsive to my people." [39]

Yes, scaling means keeping a lot of plates spinning! It can be daunting, and I have seen companies lose focus and identity along the way. In those moments, remember this: When you created your business, you knew the values that guided it. You knew your company's purpose. You had a clear idea of what your office environment looked like. You cared about the people who were with you from the beginning of this adventure.

Essentially, nothing has changed. If you find that you are straying away from any of this, you are not scaling in the right way – time to regroup!

KEY #2:
PREPARE YOU AND YOUR COMPANY FOR THE NEXT (BOLD) ITERATION.

As I said earlier, there's opportunity everywhere – when it comes to the marketplace and also when you are considering exit or succession planning. Here are some clarifying terms and concepts to get you started:

An exit typically means that the owner sells the business to a third party, and could involve a variety of moves, such as: direct sale to another owner, sale to a PE (private equity) firm, (M&A (merger and acquisition), management or employee buyout or transfer of ownership to an individual like a family member. You may be looking for a retirement exit, a great opportunity that would be lucrative for you and your company's growth, or a profitable sale that either allows you to exit or stay on in some exec/advisory capacity.

In my case, I made a plan to exit my printing company in 2007 and exited in 2010. I was in my forties at the time; I was not interested in retirement but to change my career. As you know, I had worked out a creative partnership for growth and profitability reasons, and it happily turned out to be the vehicle for my exit (with a lot of planning, positioning and negotiating to make that happen).

Succession planning, in my experience, means to look at the next iteration of your company, its plan for the future and for the next generation. What does succession planning look like? In what ways will your business live beyond your exit?

Visionary Action Step #2:
Do the inside work to prepare yourself.

- What have I been thinking about lately?
- *Where do I want my business to go? What's it going to look like?*
- *Would I want a merger, a sale, a retirement, or closing it down altogether?*
- *Will I ever be able to let this business go?*
- *Who will run things when I'm gone?*
- *How do I know when the time is right?*

These are the kinds of questions that keep many of my clients up at night. And they are good ones for the soul-searching it takes to prepare you for your company's next iteration.

1) Outline the future you want to create for yourself and your family. As you undoubtedly know by now, an important part of any bold move is what you want your life to look like in the next several years, and I hope you continue to use this book and worksheets (or call me!) to guide you. In the exercise of exit or succession, you get really specific in order to lay out the options you can work toward.

It could be helpful to create two to three scenarios to help you gain clarity and detail on the options in front of you. Say you decide you want to sell in seven years. Visualize the situation, where you'll be at that point, how your business will be functioning, and an estimate of your annual revenue (remember, we make the best analyses and decisions we can based on the info we have. The alternative is procrastination!). One thing that likely will become clear is what you DO NOT want – which is helpful!

2) *Inform yourself about the various options* so you can position your company to meet any opportunity that may arise. The best way to do this is to ask those who know or have been there already! Use your Transformational Ties to help inform your plans and decisions. Ask questions about the market climate, and where the best options and opportunities lie. Gather data.

Louis Naviasky is Founder and CEO of LAN Ventures, and has personally gone through the business selling and buying process. He finds what I've been calling Transformational Ties to be "extremely pivotal" in looking for his next iteration. "I find people to talk to from some of my senior leaders, and leverage relationships from the past [to learn what I can]. And I use LinkedIn as a free platform to put myself out there to create interest and connect with potential opportunities. I realized how important LinkedIn can be as a tool, because it's really about my personal branding." [40]

This is a great tip, dovetailing perfectly into what we talked about in Chapter Three about being an influencer. Not only can you learn about the various processes and opportunities for exiting and succession, you are also able to position yourself as a company of interest in this vast networking field.

3) *Begin the conversation with your inner circle.* Select the people you trust – whether from your kitchen cabinet, mentors, friends, family, or exec team – to help you gather information and perspective.

Louis Naviasky shared with me another important aspect of bringing in others: Put in place a solid management or leadership team "from a pool of eight to ten people who are cohesive and offer you a second tier of knowledge." These people will help you position yourself and the company for your next iteration – and also be your team when you seriously begin to take action.

Visionary Action Step #3:
Do the foundational work to prepare your company.

This follows closely with the actions you would take if you were to decide to scale – the difference is the lens through which you plan those actions. Your lens now, according to Alex Simpson, is "to get optimal evaluation of your business." Here are what he and other experts I've interviewed suggest:

1) ***Get your "back office" finances in shape.*** Make sure they are accurate and up to date. Make them as structured and transparent as possible so a buyer will have an easy time analyzing your valuation. It may be helpful to work with your accountant or with a consultant who is experienced in the vehicles you're considering, such as someone who works in/with PE, M&A, or succession planning.

Louis Naviasky suggests developing a relationship with an investment banker: "I often speak to my investment banker about how we are going to market our company for sale: What is the market looking for? What do I need to do to best position my company? Often they have the closest insight to what a buyer is looking for because they see the ins and outs in the context of the market ecosystem."

2) ***Strengthen your marketing position; build a strong brand.*** From the information you've gathered, hone your position and your message. For example, you might find out that your current target market could be tweaked to better meet the market needs you discovered from your research or advice from your investment banker. You would tailor your sales and marketing with more focus on that market, and begin to create the story you want to tell the eventual buyer about the potential and growth of your company.

3) *Put in place a strong management structure.* A buyer wants to know that your company will survive beyond you. If you haven't done so yet, THIS is the time to start delegating and developing leaders in your organization.

Why is this important? If all the power and responsibility rests on you, the CEO, it isn't going to instill confidence that your company's value is sustainable, whether or not it's for a sale, merger, partnership or management buyout. Can your leadership and teams – a company's biggest asset – carry on without you? You want the answer to be YES.

Tracey Figurelli is a Director with Andra Partners LLC a buy-side mergers and acquisitions origination firm focusing on middle-market companies. She works with private equity clients on refining and defining their acquisition strategy, and then helping them align with target companies. Tracey gives us a window into what PE and M&A companies are looking for:

"I look first at the management team: Who are these individuals? What vision do they have? How do they work with others? If I really believe in them, I take the next steps: What is their product? What's their go-to-market? Then we look at the financials of course, but our goal is to dig out those unique pieces that will differentiate the company. It could be intellectual property, the leadership team, manufacturing or distribution networks – so many different things that make that business valuable." [41]

KEY #3:
NEXT-LEVEL MOVES – MAKING YOUR EXIT AND CREATING YOUR LEGACY.

Covering all the options of a "next move" would fill another book, so my goal here is to offer some tips to help you prepare for making the important decisions and to start the processes that will take you to the ultimate evolution of your business. These are the considerations I discuss with my clients when a new venture comes into view.

Visionary Action Step #4:
Bring your company along with you – carefully.

As I mentioned earlier, here is where your trusted management team of eight to ten people becomes invaluable:

- ***Bring your team on early in the process.*** They understand your company, know the stakes, and share the vision forward so you are not going this alone. They also deserve to know the context of the moves you are looking for, and will advise you all along the way toward a successful outcome.

- ***Your team will be a powerful, united face and voice for your buyer/partner.*** All of you will represent the story of your company, its brand, growth and potential. You will know and share, as Tracey Figurelli says, what differentiates your company from others that makes your business so valuable.

- ***Your team will help manage the expectations of your people.*** To quote Yogi Berra, "It's not over 'til it's over." The reality is that deals go south for any number of reasons. Navigating these deals can demand a lot of time, resources, and energy from you and your people – it causes a significant disruption in your company, and a devastating blow when a deal falls apart.

It is up to you to manage everyone's expectations as well as your own, to keep business going as usual while leading a change effort. You and your management team can frame the conversation with your people while keeping the confidences that need to be kept to avoid unnecessary fear and anxiety.

Once a deal has been made, there will likely be transitions to handle which you and your management team can navigate together.

Visionary Action Step #5:
Consider timing and fit.

Following the steps I've outlined in this chapter will equip you to assess the offer you're looking at.

1) Is this move right for your business at this time? One thing is for sure...timing is everything.

When I was running Slater Graphics, you might remember that I looked to merge with another company. The owner and I had some great conversations, then we shook hands and walked away saying the time was not right – their personal and business goals and mine were not aligned at that time to create the merger we each envisioned.

A few years later, the timing was different. We went on to work together for over a dozen years very successfully because the mutual benefits were there. We were able to expand our people and market opportunities (and... this partnership became my exit vehicle. Thank you, LG, for a great run).

To help decide whether or not the timing might be right for a particular deal, consider:

- You: Am I ready, does this feel right? Who am I after the sale? Will I leave with more money than I would be making if I didn't take this action? Do I want a full exit, or retain a position in the leadership?
- Your company: What does the market look like in terms of eval-uating this deal – should we go forward or wait? Is the economic evaluation of the company right at this juncture? Is my leadership ready (to make this change or take over for me)?

2) Determine if this new venture is going to be a cultural fit. Or-ganizations need to be aligned to be successful. Here are areas to look at:

- Your people: What will happen to them? Would you need to expand or condense your team? Do they have the best chance of growth from this deal, not only economically but in terms of their careers?
- Your systems and operations: Where do they overlap? Are there areas where they do not gel? What will you need to invest in? How will the core values and policies change as a result of this deal?
- In a merger or equity purchase, what is the future governance going to look like? Who will be sitting at the table with you in terms of leadership and boards?

Visionary Action Step #6:

Once you decide to enter into negotiations on any deal – whether a merger, sale, VC partnership, or succession – consider these tips:

1) *Talk through money in detail.* It's not just about what is said, it is about what is shown. Ask for, and look at, proof of the numbers. Review them with your financial advisors. Look at their overhead, your overhead, the potential profitability and growth strategies. Do the numbers make sense for both of you? They in turn will be doing the same, and you already know your financial records are up to date, accurate, concise and ready for them to easily analyze!

2) *Your contract is key.* You have assets you want to protect as you go into any deal. For me, it was my clients. I had a line drafted in the contract that my clients would remain my clients, even if the partnership failed. This was non-negotiable for me. Be ready to identify what is important to protect before you go into negotiations.

3) *Align your values.* Are you and the other party on the same page with the big things, including core business principles and family values? This one area has been a reason that deals fall apart. A misalignment in values will not bring success.

Listen to your gut and your instincts. When you built your business, you had a goal in mind. Maybe you never thought about selling, merging, or any other legacy plan, but now you've found yourself in front of that opportunity. Stay true to your initial values and only align yourself with people whom you trust, respect and see yourself growing with for years to come.

Think about the short and long-term benefits of the deal. Look at every angle. Ensure you are going in with a clear mind and an open heart.

You can always walk away...toward the next opportunity!

The Ultimate Evolution of You and Your Company: TAKEAWAYS

The time to think in legacy terms is NOW (at whatever age you may be). Thinking in legacy terms sets you on a course of intentionally and actively building your company through the lens of the future. Your vision, strategic plans, decisions and actions guide you steadily toward creating your future life. What you plant today you will reap tomorrow.

Scale your company for greater profitability.

- Your vision should be limitless. As you implement your initial plans, you get continued insights on where your vision and strategy meet, and then you make adjustments and welcome the shifts.
- Keep up with your plan with a triple-A method: ASSESS, ANALYZE, ADJUST.
- Scale your team: Bring in new people while preserving your culture.

Prepare you and your company for the next (BOLD) iteration.

- Know your terms: Exit typically means selling to a third party; succession means to look at the next iteration of your company, its plan for the future and for the next generation.
- Do the inside work to prepare yourself.
- Do the foundational work to prepare your company.

Make the next-level moves – creating your exit and your legacy.

- Bring your company along with you – carefully.
- Consider timing and fit. *Is this move right for your business at this time? Is it with the right organization?*
- Be bold yet protect yourself and your company.

CONCLUSION

**y 10 o'clock meeting this morning is with Lawrence**, a relatively new client. He asks, *Well, what's on our agenda?*

Me: *Today we want to review your Q1 goals. I know this has been a year of personal challenges with your mom's surgeries – I'm so glad she's doing well! Now, it's important to get back on track and look at your numbers to prepare for a strong new year. So, I'd like to see last year and year to date. I want to see what's on your receivables. And I want to look at the hours people are doing. Then we'll spend a few minutes to discuss those reports.*

Lawrence: [Pause...] *Oh...right... let me have my team pull this together for you.*

We have done some great work so far and his company is making progress toward the goals he'd outlined to me in the beginning of our engagement. Now it's time to read his numbers story on a regular basis, objectively and critically, to start making the big things happen – otherwise known as **accountability.**

This is the point where I push my clients out of the nest with some tools to fly.

And now you and I are at the same juncture.

My hope is that I have reached you in the same way I reach my clients, to help bring you some important shifts to your mindset and practical tools for best-of-the-best success!

And because I'm all about action and accountability, let's make some notes here on your experience reading this book and what you are going to do next – your final worksheet. First...

Final thoughts

Here is the bottom line for the Visionary Leader at any stage of expansion:

- The beginning of your journey taught you many lessons. Keep those close and learn from every single one.
- Be the leader who delegates and still knows exactly what kind of money is going in and out. Don't be a leader who doesn't know their monthly revenue because they delegated all their financials.
- Be the leader who cares about, understands and takes the time to connect. Don't be a leader who doesn't spend time getting to know the people building the business with them.
- Be the leader who embraces your values with people in and outside of the office and is 100% committed to them. Don't be a leader who spends so much time at the office that they are not present with their family and friends, and misses out on the daily joys of life.
- Be the leader who always wants to be a better one – the best of the best!

AHAs and Accountability Worksheet

INSTRUCTIONS: Instead of filing away this book on your (virtual) business bookshelf, leverage your learning – and success – by completing this worksheet.

1. What are 2-3 light-bulb moments you experienced in this book?

_____

_____

_____

2. What are the top 5 concepts/tools you feel were most impactful for you?

_____

_____

_____

3. Now, what are you going to do about them? What 3 actions are you going to take from reading this book? Examples: Monthly meetings with my leadership team to report our numbers; reassessing our sales department's 'solution conversations'; hiring a new accountant who meets our needs; assembling my kitchen cabinet; working on my Big Bold Vision or Business Growth Game Plan.

_____

_____

_____

4. What do I need to know and do to hold myself accountable? Commitment motivates accountability. Answer these questions:

    •   What is my commitment to myself?

    _____

    _____

    _____

    •   What is my commitment to my company?

    _____

    _____

    _____

    •   What are 3 measures of accountability I can commit to carrying out TODAY?

    _____

    _____

    _____

HOW TO WORK WITH IVY

SLATER SUCCESS

Strategic Growth • Leadership Development • Succession Planning

Who We Are

Slater Success is a consulting and training firm that works with service-based businesses — including law firms, financial firms, and growth-minded professional companies — to strengthen leadership, align teams, and drive long-term, sustainable success. We specialize in helping organizations scale with purpose, prepare for succession, and lead with clarity.

What We Deliver:
Results That Drive Growth and Legacy

1. **Increased Revenue and Strategic Growth**
   Measurable improvements in profitability and long-term scalability

2. **Decision-Making Clarity and Vision Alignment**
   Unified leadership focused on shared goals and strategic direction

3. **Confident, Capable Leadership at All Levels**
   Stronger executive presence, communication, and follow-through

4. **Aligned Leadership Teams and Partnerships**
   Cohesive leadership culture that supports growth and collaboration

5. **Improved Communication Across Teams and Clients**
   Better collaboration, stronger relationships, and reduced friction

6. **Succession Planning That Protects the Future**
   Structures in place for smooth leadership transitions and legacy-building

7. **Support Through M&A and Business Transitions**
   Confident navigation of mergers, acquisitions, and structural shifts

8. **Better Work. Better Life**
   Clients lead with purpose — and build teams that support long-term success

Let's Start a Conversation

If you're scaling, restructuring, or preparing for the future — let's talk. We bring the clarity, alignment, and strategic support that leaders need to succeed.

✉ ivy@slatersuccess.com

🌐 www.slatersuccess.com

✍ www.linkedin.com/in/ivyslater/

ACKNOWLEDGMENTS

There are so many people to thank who had an influence on my life both personally and professionally, as well as on this book. I wouldn't be here and I couldn't have gotten this massive undertaking done without you. I'll call out a few.

Bettyanne, you are the most phenomenal co-writer. The joy and common values we share have made this book and this process a treasure that I have truly enjoyed. Anybody who knows me well knows I hate writing, so thank you for that. Thank you also for seeing the light in me, for capturing my words (making sure they're in English) and communicating my thoughts and ideas with clarity, so my message can help make an impact on the world. I am forever grateful.

Sarah, this book wouldn't have started or been here today without your driving force of saying, *Ivy, there's another book in you. We're going to get it done; we're going to make it happen!* Against all my pushback and resistance, you saw the importance of my work and my vision for it, and held me accountable in getting the *Best of the Best* out there today. For our relationship and our friendship, I am forever grateful.

Now I'll start at the beginning, because I wouldn't be here without the guidance, influence and love of my parents, Rita and Irv, and the vision they held for me. I can never put into words how much I treasure their belief in me, even when I doubted myself. They saw I was smart even when I struggled in school. They believed I was talented when I didn't see my talent. They drove me to classes during days, nights and weekends, putting my dance dreams as the priority because they were important to me. From traveling to performances to flying to London when I was sixteen, they never questioned, always supported! They taught me to show up with an open heart and an open mind. My parents saw my potential and helped me see the positive and potential in myself. You will forever be missed, and always be with me in my heart.

To my husband, Michael: You made a promise to me in my young twenties that you would always encourage, believe in me, and never stop me from doing anything I wanted to do. When I started on this crazy chapter in my life in 2007, to throw away a successful printing company and build an entirely new career—in an industry almost no one had ever heard of—you believed I could do it more than I believed it myself. Through my travels you have supported me. Meeting so many of my clients over the years, you have shared an open heart and open mind, and helped encourage and been excited for every person that I've brought through our doors. You have held me while I cried and laughed with me in joy, and always assured me with your "We got this; it's going to be fine." During trying times and successes, we've been in this journey together. Your belief has helped me believe and to see a vision and a future. I thank you and I love you.

To my kids: I know you sometimes roll your eyes when Mommy talks business, gives advice, and wants to counsel you on your careers. My clients and friends get a laugh from it too. "Hey, What do I know? I'm only your mother..." Thank you both for letting me ask numerous questions, always being there for me, for accepting the ton of love I have for you and sharing that love back to me. I treasure the journey we are all sharing together. And thank you for bringing amazing partners into our lives, expanding our family with another daughter and another son. I love all four of you.

To my granddaughter, Sydney: You get your own little paragraph as you are the light of all of our lives. Time with you reminds me of the importance of the balance in life, making time for everything that is important—family, friends, clients, team. You inspire me to practice what I often preach: Take care of yourself so you can always be there for those you love. You remind me (when I can sometimes forget) how wonderful it was when my own children were growing up like you are. Sydney, you are a joy, you are my bright shining star, you are my laughter, you are my smile, you are my heart.

This book would not be possible, or relevant, if not for the hundreds of clients I have worked with over the past seventeen years—the thousands of relationships with business colleagues and leaders with whom I have been fortunate to connect, know and build relationships. It is an immense joy to be invited into a part of your journey. From every person I connect with, I learn something and will always continue to learn. I appreciate each and every one of you. This includes the Slater Success team! Our weekly Monday morning meetings make all the wheels turn and make happen the wonderful things we do as a company. As we all know, most of this would not happen without all of you! The basis of a great company is the team, and I am forever grateful to all of you, including all the details and lift you did to support *Best of the Best* in getting out to its public.

Last but not least, to my longstanding business partner in crime I refer fondly to as LG: I have learned so much working with you over a decade. I learned the importance of what it is to have common values when you build a company; and with those values and shared respect, anything can be built. What we did in the printing industry was unprecedented (and confused a lot of our peers and colleagues) yet we did it because we knew it was right. And it worked. All the way back to 1997, we broke some rules, created our own path, and built not just a successful business but a relationship, a friendship and a family that will always be cherished in my heart. Thank you for taking that meeting back in the day from our mutual friend Barry. Thank you for saying no to me that first time, and thank you for taking that other meeting all those years later—to create an amazing organization and an amazing legacy.

REVIEWS

Frank Rekes – Partner & Financial Planner

www.PalmWealthPartners.com

You won't want to put this down once you start. Ivy talks about many things we've heard before, but says it in a way that prompts us to act. Now. Talking about alignment, our human connection and our x-factor, all things that allow us to stand out in a sea of sameness are what will excite you to dig deeper. Also having the worksheets to focus on will make the efforts worthwhile to your future success. Cause what got you here, won't get you there.

Frank King – The Mental Health Comedian

Ivy Slater's Best of the Best: Lead Boldly, Scale Rapidly, Create Your Legacy is a great and fast read, as she has the gift of bringing every day, mundane advice to life. It is a powerhouse guide for leaders eager to elevate their businesses and lives (and what leaders aren't). Slater combines personal anecdotes with actionable strategies, offering a roadmap (that would put Google Maps to shame), to align business success with personal fulfillment. Her emphasis on visionary leadership, confidence-building, and strategic financial planning resonates long after you've turned the last page.

Kelly Rittenberry Culhane

Managing Partner & Chief Growth Officer

CM Law

Working with Ivy and her team has been a transformative experience for our firm. Her unique approach goes well beyond consulting – Ivy is a corporate therapist who helped our firm navigate challenges and scale new heights. Best of the Best is a must read as it captures the essence of Ivy's wisdom and practical strategies that will profoundly impact how you lead. Highly recommended for anyone seeking to grow both personally and professionally.

Leslee Cohen – Founder All Rise Legal Counsel

Ivy Slater has been my business coach since 2022. In that time, my boutique corporate law firm has doubled in revenue and grown from three employees to thirteen. As I read this book, I nodded along in recognition of all that we have accomplished together. Best of the Best ties the lessons together—from the identification of my vision, which drives me to jump out of bed every morning, to the intense focus on the numbers that Ivy continuously reminds me will result in financial satisfaction and independence.

I am incredibly happy for all of you who get to read this book but also INCREDIBLY JEALOUS! By reading Best of the Best, I promise you will learn to build a business that fulfills your hopes and dreams.

Precious L. Williams – CEO, The Perfect Pitch Group

When I tell you that this book is a GODsend, it is! As an entrepreneur, I am always going against the grain, taking my vision for BOLD ideas to completion. When I was by myself, this seemed like the way to go. I could depend on myself and know it would be handled. The funny thing is we started to grow beyond my capability and things had to change! How do I lead, find and hire the right people, and trust I am equipped to grow and scale? My fears and insecurities crept in. Can I really do this? Is there a book on growing and scaling for me, first generation, successful, yet leading and trusting others too? I can't do everything by myself any more. That's why Ivy Slater's new book, "Best of the Best" is worth its weight in gold, heck platinum!!!!!

When you read this book, it will answer those questions you are afraid to ask your coach and others. How do you build a company and a life worth living? How do you set the tone of excellence?

How do you get into the right rooms without coming from wealth or power or deep connections? It's in this book. There are times when reading this book, I shouted out loud! Those challenges I have in my managing style, building momentum and steam while gaining rabid clients, customers and fans.

It's not easy yet Queen Ivy makes it easier and digestible to understand. She does not sugar coat. From the first few pages until the last, get ready for a treat. Never boring, always on point, straight fire!

You can do this and her worksheets are a gem in themselves to get your mind and heart going! Success is for those willing to do the work and play at a higher level while also building a life of their dreams.

EXPERT CONTRIBUTIONS & SOURCES

1   Joe Curcillo, Strategic Advisor with Generalist's Advantage Strategies LTD. https://joecurcillo.com/

2   Kevin Wolf, CFO at American Financial Exchange. https://theafex.com/company/

3   Willie Jolley, Hall of Fame Motivational/Inspirational Speaker and author. https://www.williejolley.com/

4   Mary Ann Pierce, Founder and CEO of MAP Digital https://www.linkedin.com/in/mary-ann-pierce-nyc/ and AwakenHub Global Ambassador. https://mapdigital.com/

5   Sarah Victory and Linda McCabe, How to Be Powerful: Insider Secrets to Brilliant Leadership, Sales, and Speaking. First Edition Design Publishing, FL, 2018. See also: https://www.thevictorycompany.com.

6   Aditya Mishra, General Partner of BAT VC. https://bat-vc.com/

7   Jennifer Yousem, Founder and CEO of I Heart EBITDA, https://iheartebit-da.com/.

8   Gloria Mark, Daniela Gudith and Ulrich Klocke, "The cost of interrupted work: more speed and stress." (CHI '08: Proceedings of the SIGCHI Conference on Human Factors in Computing Systems: April 6, 2008), 107-110. https://dl.acm.org/doi/10.1145/1357054.1357072

9   Laura Held, Partner at Shamrock Capital. https://shamrockcap.com/team/

10   Best Buddies International. https://www.bestbuddies.org/

11   Joi Gordon, cofounder of Rapport Inc. https://www.linkedin.com/in/joi-gordon-3b73bb2/ and Gordon Hewes Consulting. https://www.gordon-hewes.com/

12   Nina Marino, Partner at Kaplan Marino. https://kaplanmarino.com/nina-marino

13   "Four Seasons Hotels and Resorts Named 'Great Place to Work Legend' Honouring 20 Consecutive Years on Fortune's '100 Best Companies to Work For' List." Business Insider Newswire, March 9, 2017. https://markets.businessinsider.com/news/stocks/four-seasons-hotels-and-resorts-named-great-place-to-work-legend-honouring-20-consecutive-years-on-fortune-s-100-best-companies-to-work-for-list-1001819744

14   Charlotte Hu. "Why Writing by Hand is Better for Memory and Learning." Scientific American, February 21, 2024. https://www.scientificamerican.com/article/why-writing-by-hand-is-better-for-memory-and-learning/#:~:text=A%20recent%20study%20in%20Frontiers%20in%20Psychology,for%20movement%2C%20vision%2C%20sensory%20processing%20and%20memory.

15   Beth Dahle, Cofounder of Impact 100 Philadelphia https://impact-100philly.org/.

16   Stacy Francis, CEO of Francis Financial, https://www.linkedin.com/in/stacy-francis/ and Founder Savvy Ladies, https://www.savvyladies.org/.

17   Peter G. Rupport, Limitless: Nine Steps to Launch Your One Extraordinary Life. Credo House Publishers, Grand Rapids, MI, October 1, 2020.

18   Lawrence Perkins, Founder and CEO of SierraConstellation Partners, management consulting and advisory. https://sierraconstellation.com/team/lawrence-perkins/#:~:text=Lawrence%20Perkins%2C%20Founder%20and%20Chief,experience%20with%20companies%20undergoing%20transition

19   Corey S. Kupfer, Founder and Managing Partner at Kupfer, PLLC. https://www.kupferlaw.com/corey-kupfer

20   Laura Held, Partner at Shamrock Capital. https://shamrockcap.com/team/

21   Susan L. Combs, CEO of Combs & Company, LLC, https://combsandco.com/, and Founder of Pancakes for Roger, Inc., a Veterans non-profit. https://pancakesforroger.org/

22   John Wallis, Chair at Rule No.1 sustainable consulting, and former Global Leader of Key Strategic Initiatives at Hyatt

23   Ron Alvesteffer, President and CEO of Service Express. https://serviceexpress.com/

24   Susan Graham, President of Susan Graham Consulting LLC. https://susangconsulting.com/

25   Nancy Rizzuto, Founding Partner and Principal, CAP STRAT. https://www.capstratig.com/

26   Susan L. Combs, CEO of Combs & Company, LLC, https://combsandco.com/, and Founder of Pancakes for Roger, Inc., a Veterans non-profit. https://pancakesforroger.org/

27   Nicola "Nikki" Fraser, Managing Partner and Cofounder, NextKey Services. https://www.nextkeyservices.com/

28   Joi Gordon, cofounder of Rapport Inc. https://www.linkedin.com/in/joi-gordon-3b73bb2/ and Gordon Hewes Consulting. https://www.gordon-hewes.com/

29   Dale Carnegie, How to Win Friends & Influence People. Gallery Books, imprint of Simon & Schuster, New York City, 1998.

30   Mary Ann Pierce, Founder and CEO of MAP Digital https://www.linkedin.com/in/mary-ann-pierce-nyc/ and AwakenHub Global Ambassador. https://mapdigital.com/

31   Michele Mirman, Senior Partner and Founder, Mirman, Markovits & Landau, P.C. https://mirmanlawyers.com/

32   Barbara Yong, partner at Golan Christie Taglia LLP. https://gct.law/

33   Corey S. Kupfer, Founder and Managing Partner at Kupfer, PLLC. https://www.kupferlaw.com/corey-kupfer

34   Roger Connors and Tom Smith, The Wisdom of Oz: Using Personal Accountability to Succeed in Everything You Do." Portfolio Publishers, an imprint of Penguin Group (USA). 2014.

35   Stacy Francis, CEO of Francis Financial, https://www.linkedin.com/in/stacy-francis/ and Founder Savvy Ladies, https://www.savvyladies.org/.

36   Beth Haggerty, Executive, Entrepreneur, Board Member, Advisor. https://www.linkedin.com/in/haggertybeth/

37   Maurissa Bell, Private Equity Investor. https://www.linkedin.com/in/maurissa-bell-cpa-ca-1a7o6214/

38   Alex S. Simpson, cofounder and Chair of LiquidLP. https://www.getliquidlp.com/

39   Ariana Tadler, Founder and Managing Partner, and E-Discovery strategist, Tadler Law LLP. https://www.tadlerlaw.com/

40   Louis Naviasky, Founder and CEO of LAN Ventures. https://www.linkedin.com/company/lan-ventures/

41   Tracey Figurelli, Director at Andra Partners, LLC. https://www.andrapartners.com/professionals.html

ABOUT THE AUTHOR

Ivy Slater is CEO of Slater Success, where she works with hundreds of CEOs, particularly in the service industry arena, to lead, build and scale their businesses. Drawing on her 25+ years of sales savvy honed on the unforgiving streets of Manhattan, Ivy's combination of consulting and coaching can boost results up to 40% in six months or less. What sets her apart from others is her expertise not just in the strategic nuts and bolts of financials, sales, operations and marketing that achieve rapid growth, but also in the crucial leadership inner game of confidence, honest influence, clear communication, and transformational relationship building.

Ivy is a lifelong entrepreneur, international best-selling author, and podcast host. She speaks nationwide in corporate environments on the topics of leadership, sustainable growth, and succession planning. She is living her best life in the heart of Manhattan with her husband, enjoying dining out, going to shows, traveling often, and being with her children and grandchildren.

www.ingramcontent.com/pod-product-compliance
Lightning Source LLC
Chambersburg PA
CBHW061741120626
46550CB00005B/1847